For the menders,
the makers,
and my family
(who are both)

HOW TO KEEP YOUR CLOTHES FOREVER

How to Keep Your Clothes Forever

Leah Giblin

with photography by Bee Elton

Simple planet-friendly projects to love your wardrobe back to life

Smith Street Books

CONTENTS

INTRODUCTION

I grew up with the best collection of dress-up clothes. The old, red, tin box was full of my mum's hippie dresses and boots from the 1960s and '70s. The light cotton dresses with silver threads running through them, still smelling of incense, were glorious and sparkly. We could do whatever we wanted with them. I spent hours playing dress-ups with my siblings, styling them (somewhat forcefully) into the characters of our made-up worlds. (That's me in the hat and gloves.)

I learned to sew by cutting up and remaking the dress-ups into clothes for myself. I made and remade them until the only bits left were threadbare patches, which I sewed onto other clothes as decorations or mending.

I still have that dress-up box today, along with a love of working with what I have. Instead of buying new clothes, I reinvent the clothes I already own. If they get stained, I dye them a colour that hides the stains. If I'm loving short hems for a season, I hem all my pants short, then take them down the year after. Originating from necessity, this philosophy remains one I live by. I love my existing clothes to death before I buy new ones.

My story

I've always loved sewing and making my own clothes. I've also always cared deeply about environmental issues. After blockading against uranium mines in the late 1990s, I completed a degree in environmental studies and worked in that field for a short time. It wasn't long before I found myself craving a career with more creativity, so I enrolled in a costume-making degree. After graduating, I worked in film and television costume departments on movies like *The Great Gatsby*, *The Wolverine* and *The Chronicles of Narnia: The Voyage of the Dawn Treader*.

Once I had children, I found it impossible to keep working in the film industry due to the long hours. I also started to feel like I was contributing to an ever-increasing waste problem. I was constantly dreaming of ways to combine my two great loves: textiles and sustainability. My parents had introduced me to natural dyeing as a young child; I started experimenting with this and created the first few designs of a sustainable clothing range. My friends at Cornersmith Café invited me to teach workshops in creating natural dyes using their food waste, and the rest is history. My clothing brand Day Keeper was born and my dream of combining textiles and sustainability had become a reality.

These days, I'm a textile and clothing designer, educator and sustainable fashion advocate. I work with incredible dancers and craftspeople, and collaborate on textile and costume projects with contemporary artists and curators to create large-scale textile artworks and costumes.

I create sustainability workshops for local councils and museums, and run my sustainable clothing label and mending business from my studio on Gadigal Land in Sydney, Australia.

I'm also the mother of two beautiful kiddos, whom I'm raising to be eco-warriors of the future.

The textile waste problem

Although fashion is an important space for creativity and can be so much fun, it also has a dark side: waste, pollution and exploitation. Clothes left over from fleeting trends often end up in landfill when consumers move on to their next obsession. Every second, the equivalent of one rubbish truck full of clothes is burned or dumped in a landfill.[1] That's 10 rubbish trucks of clothes waste dumped in the time it's taken you to read this. It's too much! Too many clothes are being made and there is too much waste. The fashion manufacturing industry is a big polluter. Fashion production makes up 10% of humanity's carbon emissions and is the second-largest consumer of water worldwide.[2]

We are buying far more clothing than we need and disposing of it at a great rate. Many of these garments are low quality, being produced unethically from fabrics derived from petrochemicals, then dumped on developing countries after a single wear. It's a huge problem that can feel too big to tackle. This book focuses on positive solutions to guide us out of this mess. I plan to show you how to advocate for a fashion industry that's healthy for the people who make it, for animals and for the planet.

How to use this book

This book aims to help you apply the 'dress-up box' philosophy to your own life, inspire excitement for making the most of what you have, and encourage you to care for and reinvent your clothes so they'll last you a lifetime.

It will help you to fall (back) in love with the clothes you already own. When you decide it's time to buy something new, this book will arm you with the knowledge to make empowered, truly sustainable and ethical choices.

The book is divided into three sections with projects to help guide you towards responsible clothing stewardship:

Section 1: Buy Less
encourages you to analyse your reasons for buying clothing.

Section 2: Care
shows you how to look after your precious garments.

Section 3: Keep
teaches you how to revolutionise the items you already own.

You can use this book as a quick reference guide for each stage of owning a garment or as a workbook to go through at your own pace. Along with instructions for mending and repairs, practical projects in each section will show you how much usable fabric there is in used clothes, bedding and upholstery fabrics that would usually be thrown away. Each project has step-by-step instructions and suggestions for what to upcycle for fabric.

What does clothing stewardship mean?

Buying an item of clothing means taking responsibility for the lifetime of the garment in partnership with the brand that produced it. The clothing you buy remains your responsibility even after it leaves your care. Even when made from natural fibres, garments can last a VERY long time: the oldest surviving garment, the Tarkhan Dress, found in a tomb in Egypt, is believed to be more than 5000 years old.

So, before you buy, you need to decide whether the garment is worth the responsibility. Polyester clothing can take anywhere from 20 to 200 years to decompose.[3] That's a long time to care for a garment. Where it ends up, whether in landfill or in someone else's wardrobe, is partly up to you. If you look after a garment while it's in your care, and learn to repair or remake it into something that extends its useful life, it's much less likely to end up in landfill. Clothing stewardship means agreeing to take responsibility for the whole life cycle of a garment when it comes into your care. If everyone applied this principle when purchasing new clothing, we'd have a lot less waste.

SECTION 1
BUY LESS

The practical reasons for owning clothes are simple. We need clothes to protect ourselves from the weather, for modesty and hygiene, and to replace what we've grown out of or worn out. Once we've met our practical needs for clothing, our motivations for buying new clothes are complex and personal. It might simply be that your eye was caught by that sparkly top in a shop window, or that you feel more confident in a new outfit. Whatever the reason, this section encourages you to analyse the why before you buy.

The projects will help you figure out how much clothing you actually need and compare it to how much you already own. Hopefully, this will encourage you to buy less. If you do need to buy, however, I'll offer alternatives to buying new and show you how to identify a quality garment that's made to last. I'll explain how to find out if something is truly made sustainably and ethically, and teach you about types of fibres. You'll figure out your own personal style, so instead of being a slave to fashion, you can make fashion work for you.

Let's get into it.

Know the why before you buy

To gain control of our shopping choices, finances and environmental impact, we need to know the reasons why we're buying. It helps to have a checklist of questions to ask yourself before you commit. The first section of this book is divided into these questions, with projects and tips included to help. If you're buying online, leave the items in your cart until you've worked through this list. If you're in a physical shop, leave it on the rack until you've figured out if you really need it.

The buying checklist

Screenshot this list and keep it on your phone.

☐ **Do you really need it?**
(see pages 18–23)

☐ **Why are you buying it?**
(see pages 24–25)

☐ **Is it a classic or fad?**
(see pages 26–33)

☐ **Does it work with three items you already own?** (see pages 36–37)

☐ **Can you find it second-hand, swap for it or hire it?**
(see pages 38–41)

☐ **Is it good quality and well made? Will it last?** (see pages 42–45)

☐ **Is it sustainably and ethically made?** (see pages 46–51)

☐ **Could you learn how to make it yourself?** (see pages 53–55)

As fashion designer and author Orsola de Castro states: 'To maintain, to keep, to repair and rewear your own clothes is the most sustainable thing you can do (when it comes to fashion of course).'[4]

The following graphic is a guideline of what to prioritise for maximum sustainability when it comes to clothes.

Use what you own: Upgrade, refresh, mend

Buy it local second-hand, swap or trade for it, hire it, or make it with second-hand fabric

Make it yourself with new fabric

Buy new: Locally made sustainable/ethical

Buy new: International sustainable/ethical

Buy new: Other (fast fashion)

CHAPTER 1: DO YOU NEED IT?

'Buy less, choose well, make it last.' —Vivienne Westwood

The fashion industry relies on convincing us that we 'need' new clothes, but how much do we really need? These two projects will help you figure this out. The clothing calculator project helps you determine your basic clothing needs and the wardrobe stocktake project helps you compare that to what you already have. Once you've completed both projects, you'll have a clear snapshot of your wardrobe, which can help you answer the following questions:

- **Do you really need what you're about to buy?**

- **Can you make better use of what you already own?**

- **Can you learn to make it yourself using fabric you already have?**

Set aside a day to complete the clothing calculator and wardrobe stocktake projects.

After completing the clothing calculator project myself, I was surprised to discover that I own 40 T-shirts and 23 woollen jumpers. That means I can go for more than a month without having to wash a single T-shirt! I had no idea I'd collected so many, as I wash and wear only three of them on repeat.

Project: Clothing calculator

Create a list of the minimum amount of clothes you need for your lifestyle. This calculator gives you a simplified snapshot of your clothing needs.

Pick a season and think of what you wear in an average week. Underneath the heading for each clothing type, list every item of ONE outfit. Add more bubbles to the table for anything you need specific clothing for. For example, if you work for five days with a two-day weekend, go out once a week and go to the gym twice a week, you'd list:

**1 average work outfit,
which might include:**

- collared shirt
- blazer
- trousers

**1 average weekend outfit,
which might include:**

- jeans
- t-shirt
- hoodie

**1 average going-out outfit ,
which might include:**

- skirt
- blouse
- casual jacket

**1 average gym outfit,
which might include:**

- leggings
- singlet

There's no need to go into specifics, just list one example of an outfit you'd wear for each activity; for example, a casual summer weekend might look like: 1 x T-shirt, 1 x shorts; and a work outfit could be: 1 x shirt, 1 x trousers, 1 x blazer.

Don't include anything you need for sentimental reasons or because it's nice to look at. This activity is to list what you need for *purely practical* purposes.

Once you've completed each bubble, add the number of days per week you do each activity. To calculate totals, multiply each item on the list by the number of days you've noted for each activity. Repeat for summer and winter if you live in a place where your outfits are seasonally dependent. Then add up the totals and you'll have a useful list of the minimum amount of clothes you could live with.

Do you need it? **19**

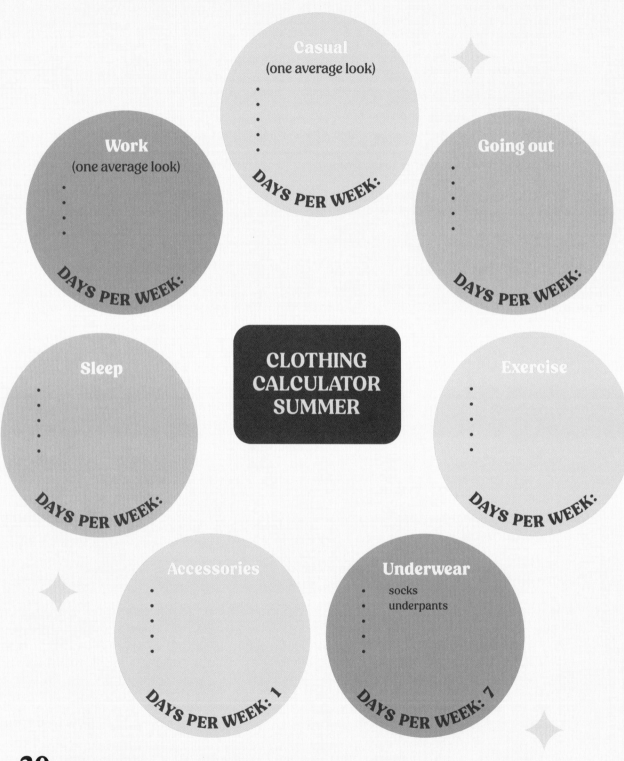

Casual
(one average look)
- .
- .
- .
- .

DAYS PER WEEK:

Work
(one average look)
- .
- .
- .
- .

DAYS PER WEEK:

Going out
- .
- .
- .

DAYS PER WEEK:

CLOTHING CALCULATOR SUMMER

Sleep
- .
- .
- .
- .

DAYS PER WEEK:

Exercise
- .
- .
- .
- .

DAYS PER WEEK:

Accessories
- .
- .
- .
- .

DAYS PER WEEK: 1

Underwear
- socks
- underpants
- .
- .
- .

DAYS PER WEEK: 7

WHAT I NEED

Work	Casual	Exercise	Going out	Underwear	Accessories
e.g. 5 x work shirts 3 x blazers 2 x trousers 1 x work skirt					
				Sleep	

<u>TOTALS</u>: To calculate totals, multiply each item in the bubble by the number of days per week you wear it.

<u>NOTE:</u> You can change these numbers based on your best judgement. With items like outerwear, blazers and suits that you aren't cleaning after each wear, you don't need as many. If you wear a suit five days a week, you probably only need two or three suits, not five. For items like underwear that you wash after each use, you might add more depending on your washing cycles. For example, one pair of underpants for each day of the week and three extra for the wash rotation, coming to 10 in total.

Do you need it? **21**

NOTE: Putting photos of your outfits beside your wardrobe can help you remember what you have and keep everything in use.

Project: Wardrobe stocktake

Here, you'll calculate how much clothing you *actually* have, which might surprise you. Perhaps you've got some items you never wear or that still have tags on them. It's easy to accumulate clothes, hiding them away in drawers and always adding more.

In the table on the next page, list every item you currently own in the relevant category. After completing the table, compare the numbers you get for the clothing calculator and wardrobe stocktake projects. If they are basically the same, well done! The amount of clothing you own doesn't exceed your basic needs. If the numbers in your wardrobe stocktake are higher, this means you already own more than you need and you don't need to shop for more.

For more on how to make better use of what you already own, after you've done your wardrobe stocktake, you can jump straight into Section 3: Keep (page 103). If you've found that your practical clothing needs are covered, yet you still have an urge to shop, keep reading this section.

NOTE: You may want to do the wardrobe revolution project in Chapter 12 'Love your wardrobe back to life' (see page 107) at the same time as the wardrobe stocktake to avoid having to empty your closet more than once.

WHAT I HAVE

Work	Casual	Exercise	Going out
e.g. 5 x shirts 2 x blazers 4 x trousers			

Sleep	Underwear	Accessories	Other

CHAPTER 2: WHY DO YOU BUY?

When it comes to fashion, 'Why do I buy?' is a powerful question. Fashion marketing works hard to obscure and override our need to ask it. But asking this question is important; it can provoke a deeper look at ourselves and our spending habits. When we know our personal motivations, we can take control over our behaviour and habits.

Whether I need it or not, I get excited about buying when I think something is a bargain. I also can't resist anything unique, vintage or handmade. Do any of these reasons resonate with you?

- Buying new clothes makes me feel better emotionally.

- I need to keep up with trends to stay relevant.

- I need to collect or complete a set.

- I feel like buying new clothes during a sale saves me money.

- Buying new clothes makes me feel like something is within my control.

- I buy to express my identity.

- I buy because I don't want to repeat outfits.

- I buy because I feel more acceptable in new clothes.

If one or more of these statements hits home, you're not alone. The fashion industry uses the *very same* reasons to keep us buying more, bombarding us with marketing to reinforce the messages 'You are not enough without new clothes' and 'You need to keep up.'

> '*Brands create demand and spend millions engineering the customer experience to get people to buy more*'[5]

The reasons why we buy are incredibly powerful, emotional drivers that cost us money, contribute to the fashion waste crisis and eventually leave us feeling worse about ourselves. The unfortunate truth is that, even if new clothes make us feel better momentarily, they won't satisfy our emotional needs for long. Within this cycle, the only way to keep feeling better is to keep buying. A shopping addiction can be as damaging and hard to shake as any other form of addiction.

What I'd love to convince you of is that it's possible for us to express our identities, feel better emotionally, add to our collections, save money and take control without buying anything new – even without buying anything at all.

If new clothes do make you feel better emotionally, it can help to write down how and why. How long does the feeling last? Does anything else give you a similar feeling? Can you do some work emotionally that would make you feel better for longer? Is there a root cause you need to address?

If you feel it's a problem that's significantly affecting your life, seek out counselling. You don't have to deal with this alone.

CHAPTER 3: CLASSIC OR FAD?

'Fashion is about knowing who you are and declaring who you want to be.' —Anna Wintour

A great way to disconnect from fashion marketing's endless messages is to know what you love, what works on you and what makes you feel great when you wear it. Drown out the noise by knowing your fit, being true to your personal style and sticking with your classics rather than following trends. This means you won't be compelled to buy on a whim because you know exactly what you're looking for and what will work with your existing wardrobe. By reducing impulse purchasing, you'll end up throwing less away.

Choose your muse

A great way to get inspired and gather ideas is by choosing a muse and starting a mood board. Find someone online with a similar shape to you and a style you love – it could be a historical figure or someone around today. What looks good on them? What parts of their outfits do you want to try? What's different about their style from how you currently dress? Make a list.

I have many mood boards on the go at one time. My current board is named 'Style icons for this phase'. In it, I've put outfits, haircuts, historical references, colour palettes, textures and accessory ideas that I love. I check it often to give myself outfit ideas and inspiration, and if I see something else I love, I add it to the board.

Find your style through play

To figure out what works for you, find time and space to *play*. Play with style, colour, pattern, fit and shape. Through play, you can change your relationship with fashion from one where the fashion industry dictates what you should wear, to one that's personally empowering and exciting.

Project: Style play

Grab a friend and go to a bricks-and-mortar clothing store, second-hand shop, clothing swap, hire shop or even a friend's house – any place with a more diverse selection of clothes than your usual scope and where you'll feel comfortable taking your time.

Do this on a day you're feeling confident and don't take it too seriously. This exercise is all about play, like dress-ups when you were a kid.

NOTE: You're not alone if shops and fitting rooms make you feel instantly uncomfortable. If a store doesn't provide clothing sizes or changing spaces that work for you in terms of accessibility, let them know that's the reason you won't be supporting their business.

Follow these steps:

- Claim a fitting room and make it comfortable for you. Cover the mirror if it makes you feel better.

- Gather a bunch of clothes that will let you play with shapes, sizes, patterns and colours outside your usual choices and your comfort zone. Where you'd usually wear oversized, try something fitted. Try a structured shoulder if you usually wear soft. And try tucking shirts in if you usually wear them out and long.

- Try some looks inspired by your muse.

- Take your time and try on at least ten outfits, getting photos of each.

LIFESTYLE

- Take photos of yourself that include your whole body from head to toe. Make sure they're shot from a consistent distance and that the lighting is good. Get a friend to help if you can't do this yourself.

- Don't buy anything yet.

- Wait at least a day before you look at the photos.

- Analyse the photos with a friend – are there unexpected items that look surprisingly good? What worked and what didn't? Are there shapes you want to adopt into your personal style permanently? Do you already own pieces that could do the same thing or could you alter something to make it work? (See Section 3: Keep, page 103.)

- Make a list of what works and refer to it before you purchase, hire or swap.

Classic or fad?

<u>NOTE:</u> Keep it positive and have fun! Taking photos helps you get perspective on what works and what doesn't. Head noise can be extremely distracting, and it's often hard to distinguish between what's in your head and what you're actually seeing. Having a friend with you when you're trying things on, and when you're looking at the photos later, will help you see yourself more objectively and cut through any negative self-talk.

STYLING TIP

Most of us try to cover up the parts of our bodies we're most unhappy with in larger clothes. It seems counterintuitive, but often these areas are where we should wear fitted clothes. For example, I have a long body and lovely short legs proportionately. In my 20s, I wore long tops or skirts over pants to try to obscure the place where my legs joined my torso. As I learned more about styling and proportion, I realised that all those long T-shirts were actually making my body look even longer and my legs shorter.

I now wear the exact opposite: high-waisted, fitted trousers and a tucked-in T-shirt so the length of my body is broken up into shorter sections and my legs are uninterrupted up to my waist. This gives the illusion of longer legs and a shorter body. As a rule, anything you cover up with a lot of fabric will look exaggerated; to counteract this, use the least amount of fabric to cover the parts you most want to hide. This styling tip sometimes has the added benefit of helping free us from not feeling good about parts of our wonderful bodies. Once we reveal our least-favourite areas, we often realise we never needed to hide them at all.

What's your fit?

To put it bluntly, garment sizing sucks and can be exclusionary. Most shops only cater for a narrow size range and display clothes on unrealistic models, when in reality our bodies are much more varied and beautiful. There is no standard measure of size and no average shape. (The fashion industry perpetuates this myth so they can churn out standard-sized clothing.) Very few people can buy clothes off the rack and have them fit perfectly. I want us to adopt an attitude of changing clothes to *fit us*, rather than changing our bodies to *fit clothes*.

Often, we stop wearing a piece of clothing with a fitting issue that has a simple solution; inevitably, this is the reason it ends up in the bin. Whatever the problem, there's a solution. It's worth figuring out because clothing should fit us, make us feel good about our bodies and be comfortable, no matter our size or shape. Don't settle for less.

On the following pages are some tips to help you find the perfect fit.

WHERE TO MEASURE

- <u>Know your measurements.</u> If you don't own a tape measure, go to your local supermarket and buy one. For accurate measurements, keep the tape horizontally straight all the way around you as you measure. Stand up straight and breathe normally as you measure; don't puff up your chest. Look straight ahead with your arms relaxed at your sides. Measuring yourself in front of a mirror helps with this, or get a friend to assist you. Write down your measurements and keep them in your phone.

- <u>Find what measurements fit.</u> Lots of brands now list the actual measurements of their garments in their online stores. Find a similar garment in your wardrobe that you love the fit of, lay it on a flat surface, and measure the width and length. Measure the waist of your favourite jeans and skirts. Save this information in your phone for easy reference.

- <u>Avoid online purchases.</u> Buying online when you can't try things on can be problematic in terms of transport and waste. We return things more often when we buy them online.[6] If you can find the same item to try on for real, you'd be saving a whole lot of waste and supporting a local business in the process.

- <u>Try clothes on before you take them home.</u> Spend time doing this, carefully analysing what works and what doesn't.

- <u>Identify recurring fit issues.</u> Some things about clothes often bother us over and over again. This could be something like your jeans always gaping at the back of your waist when they fit perfectly elsewhere, or armholes being too tight or shoulders too wide. Maybe clothing rubs you in a similar place or has a texture that irritates you. If you have something you love that fits you in most places but has one issue, don't throw it away. Take it to an alterations shop to fix the problem. If you're an aspiring maker, ask the alterations person to explain how they've done it. Maybe you could learn to do it yourself.

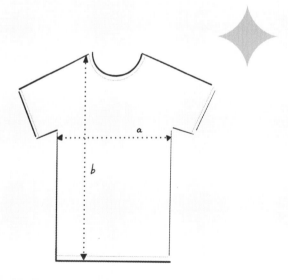

- **Help brands up their game.** Give feedback to brands with sizing that doesn't work and find which brand makes the best fit for you.

- **Create a template for fitting success.** When you find an item that fits you well, make a pattern of it or have someone make a pattern for you, so you can get multiple garments made in a shape you feel comfortable in. This might be the pattern that inspires you to take a sewing class to learn how to make your own!

Does it work with three items you already own?

Another trick to resist shopping on a whim is to make sure any item you buy works with at least three items in your existing wardrobe. This is similar to the idea of a capsule or minimalist wardrobe, where each item needs to be interchangeable with other items so you can create a variety of different looks with just a few garments.[7]

You'll find great books and websites that explain how to build a capsule wardrobe. A warning though: the term 'capsule wardrobe' is often used as a way to sell more clothes. Collections marketed as 'capsule collections', in which all pieces work together interchangeably, are just fashion collections. All fashion collections are designed to be cohesive sets. So, despite what you read, you don't need to discard everything you own and buy a completely new set of clothes to make this work. You can apply the philosophy to what you already own and use it as a guideline if you need to replace something.

The most useful idea here is interchangeability. You might love a garment at first sight and want to keep it forever, but applying the three-item rule helps you decide whether it has a functional place in your wardrobe.

This philosophy requires thought and research before a purchase, which is never a bad thing. If you spend a day workshopping which items work with others, you might find new combinations in your existing wardrobe you'd never considered. (See Chapter 17: Keep your wardrobe fresh, page 209.)

What works together depends entirely on your personal style. You may love a pattern-clash look, or you might be a minimalist. Traditionally, items in a capsule wardrobe are plain and neutral in colour to ensure they combine well with as many other items as possible and minimise the risk of a 'clash'. This doesn't need to be the case! If you have a colourful wardrobe, it makes sense to add more colour.

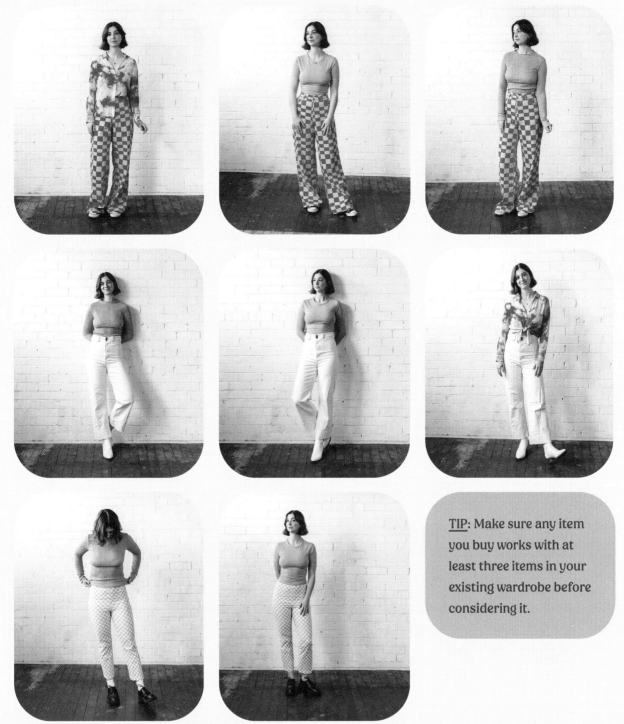

TIP: Make sure any item you buy works with at least three items in your existing wardrobe before considering it.

CHAPTER 4: COULD YOU FIND IT SECOND-HAND, SWAP FOR IT OR HIRE IT?

If you need an item of clothing and can't use something you already own, second-hand should always be your first choice. Try to resort to buying new only for things like underwear and socks – and for these items, choose locally made, well-made and organic natural fibres where possible.

The world of second-hand is full of options:

- **Local second-hand shops or online stores**
- **Hire shops**
- **Clothing swaps**
- **Trading with friends**
- **Second-hand fabric**

Second-hand shops

The second-hand clothing industry is booming, both online and in-store. Look online for your local 'buy, sell, trade' or 'pay it forward' groups for local second-hand treasures. Don't forget to follow the buying checklist (see page 16) whether it's new or second-hand. Don't buy it if you don't need it and always follow the care instructions listed on the tag.

Wear and tear

Before you buy, check common places for wear and tear: the top edges of collars, elbows, underarms, crotches and hems. If you find a special piece that fits, but has wear and tear that might be fixable, follow the repair instructions in Chapter 14: The 'Fix' pile (see pages 110–149) or take it to your local alterations business.

- **Easy-to-fix wear-and-tear issues:** Musty smells (see page 85), missing buttons (see pages 113–114), hems coming down (see pages 117–119), split seams (see pages 121–123), holes (see pages 125–139) and worn-out elastic (see pages 145–148).

- **Hard-to-fix wear-and-tear issues:** Broken zips (these can be taken to your local alterations shop to replace), worn-out collars (see pages 141–143) and thin, brittle fabric.

Check fit

If the piece is spectacular and you love it, but it has a minor fitting issue, take it to your local alterations shop to have it fitted especially to you. This is often much cheaper than you'd expect and makes use of something already in circulation. It's a much more sustainable choice than buying new.

- **Easy-to-change fitting issues:** Hem and cuff length, leg width, waist circumference.

- **Hard-to-change fitting issues:** Body length, armhole size, crotch length, making items bigger.

Check what it's made from

Second-hand synthetic garments release microplastics into our waterways when they're washed – every time, no matter their age. Polyester is common in vintage but as long as it's washed with care using a microfilter washing bag to capture microplastics, it's better to keep it in circulation than throw it out. For more on how to limit the impact of synthetics, check out Section 2: Care (see pages 57–101).

Swap

What is a clothing swap?

Clothing swaps are an organised way to make one person's trash another person's treasure. They're a terrific way to share clothes without having to spend a cent. Many established swaps are happening around the place: just search 'clothing swap near me' to see what's around. Another option is to organise your own swap. Make it as large or small as you like: set the parameters in terms of what kinds of clothes you want to swap, decide who's bringing the nibbles and voila! (For more, see 'Organise a clothing swap', pages 205–207.)

How do they work?

Whoever organises the swap decides what can be swapped. Mostly this would be good-quality outerwear, with nothing that needs mending or that you wouldn't gift to a dear friend. Sometimes you bring your bag of clothes to swap and someone checks it when you arrive. Swaps often use a token system, so after your clothes are checked, you're given the same number of tokens as items you've contributed. Then you head in and 'spend' your tokens on other people's clothes. Otherwise, swaps have an honesty system: you contribute good stuff and take away roughly the same amount of good stuff in return.

It feels amazing to offload clothes you've fallen out of love with and leave with a completely 'new to you' collection. The best part is there's no money involved, you're keeping clothes out of landfill and you haven't contributed to the waste crisis. Wins all around!

> ## CLOTHING SWAP TIP
>
> Don't forget to try things on and follow the same checklist as for buying new (see page 16). Don't get caught up in the moment and leave with things that you'll regret later. Once you've taken the items home, they're your responsibility to look after and care about where they end up, so make sure you'll love these pieces long term.

Hire

If you've got a special occasion to go to, hiring will give you bang for your buck. Often, we only wear those fancy items – like formal, bridesmaid or wedding outfits – a couple of times. Instead of buying new and having it sit in your cupboard taking up space after one hurrah, try renting a high-quality garment without having to take responsibility for the lifetime of that garment.

The pros of hiring:

- Most hire businesses take care of dry-cleaning and repairs. Check whether your local hire business prioritises green dry-cleaning methods and offsets their carbon emissions.

- Clothes are cleaned well and are hygienic.

- Items are often high quality, well made and a fraction of the cost of buying the item new.

- Hire businesses stock brands you may not be able to afford to buy new.

- You don't have the responsibility of caring for a garment for its entire lifetime, upcycling it or disposing of it when it's done.

The cons of hiring:

- Hire businesses rely heavily on dry-cleaning, which uses a lot of chemicals and energy.

- They rely on freight, which uses fossil fuels.

Most hire businesses have websites where you can search based on size, colour, occasion or style. When you can find what you need, hiring lets you party on, then hand it back.

CHAPTER 5: IS IT GOOD QUALITY AND WILL IT LAST?

Clothes look great on a hanger in a shop, but once you get them home, you find out pretty quickly which ones are made to last. Spotting the difference before you buy can save you money, keep clothes out of landfill and send a message to manufacturers about what we as consumers want.

How to spot poorly made clothing:

- **Look inside for loose threads.** If it's a mess inside, chances are the garment's been made in a hurry. Quality garments should be neatly finished and have threads snipped. If there are loose threads, check whether all seams have been sewn together properly and finished off with either binding or overlocking. If the inside seams are left raw, a garment can fray over time.

- **Gently pull seams apart.** Sometimes after you've worn something once, you'll notice the stitches holding two panels together are loose, making stitches visible on the outside of a garment. This is more common in stretch items and gets worse over time.

Examples of poorly made:

Bad overlocking   Fraying seam

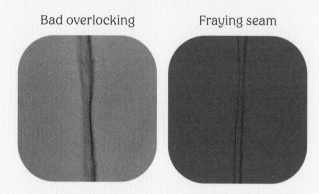

Examples of well made:

Overlocked seam   Bound seam

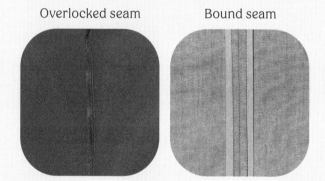

- **Check hems and cuffs.** Make sure they're stitched around the complete circumference and that the stitches look strong.

- **Check buttons.** Make sure they are sewn on firmly. Is a spare button included?

- **Feel the fabric.** Does it feel strong? Does it feel nice on your skin? Is it breathable? Natural fibres let your skin breathe, absorb sweat and are much less smelly. Synthetic fibres do and are the opposite.

- **Gently rub the fabric between your fingers.** Does the dye rub off? This is normal and expected with some kinds of indigo dyeing and denim jeans, but be careful when washing. If dye rubs off on your fingers, the colour is unlikely to last. Expect a lot of fading and wash separately. Check the tag to see if the manufacturer has warned about fading or colour-bleeding.

- **Check the zip.** Does it move smoothly and is it easy to open and close? If the zip is broken but you love the piece, take it to your local alterations shop for a new zip.

- **Will it pill after one wear?** Loose-knit fibres made from low-quality synthetics are most likely to pill. You can remove pilling, but these pieces require more upkeep than tightly knitted, quality fibres.

- **Try it on in a shop.** Online stores use all the tricks in the book to make things look great on models when they're photographing clothes. It's hard to know what will actually turn up in the post. If you can try something on in a shop, you're much less likely to return it. Walking or cycling to a real store has the lowest carbon footprint in terms of shopping.[8]

- **Check the pockets are actually pockets.** To cut corners, sometimes manufacturers will add a fake pocket front that doesn't have a pocket bag attached. This one blows my mind! It seems like they go to almost as much trouble as making an actual pocket, then you get the piece home and realise it can't be opened. Don't confuse this with the tailoring technique of stitching a tailored pocket closed. You can open tailored pockets by snipping a few small stitches.

Is it good quality and will it last? 43

How to calculate cost per wear

Calculating cost per wear isn't tricky. You take the cost of a garment, add any extra costs like alterations or mending, then divide that by how many times you've worn or are planning to wear it. For example, if I spend $300 on a jacket plus $35 on alterations to shorten the sleeves, the total cost is $335. If I plan to wear the jacket for 15 days every winter for 10 years, that's 150 wears. Divide $335 by 150 and you get a cost per wear of $2.23. If I keep and wear it for 30 years, the cost per wear is 74 cents – even better! Cost per wear calculations vary depending on what you use items for. Aim to keep your cost per wear as low as possible (ideally under $5) by choosing, keeping and rewearing clothes that will last the distance.

For something that's made to last, the cost per wear will be low. If you buy something and only wear it once, however, the cost per wear is incredibly high. Mass-produced clothing that only lasts a few washes has a high cost per wear, even if the garment was cheap to buy.

Alongside cost per wear, always consider the true cost of a garment. This includes considering the rights of the person who made the garment, as well as the garment's environmental cost.

Look for slow fashion

Slow fashion is a movement that operates in resistance to the fast-fashion model. It is based on ethical sourcing, design, production and consumption with an awareness of the social, cultural and ecological implications of garments.[9] The clothing is often based more on classic styles than fashion fads and is made as consciously as possible in every aspect. Slow fashion is mostly made to order or custom made, so there may be a waitlist, but with its emphasis on ethics, sustainability, quality construction and materials, slow-fashion garments are more likely to last you a lifetime.

CHAPTER 6: IS IT SUSTAINABLY AND ETHICALLY MADE?

Sustainability in fashion can be a pretty puzzling topic. Many brands use words like 'sustainable', 'organic' and 'eco' in their marketing, but what do these words really mean? This chapter will help you wade through the hype to figure out how sustainable a garment really is.

Greenwashing

'The act or practice of making a product, policy, activity, etc. appear to be more environmentally friendly or less environmentally damaging than it really is.'[10]

The fashion industry makes the topic of sustainability deliberately confusing. Many brands have been accused of 'greenwashing' by tricking consumers into thinking they're buying sustainable goods when they aren't.[11] If a garment is made from 10% organic cotton and 90% polyester, for example, is it still okay to use the word 'organic' in bold type on the tag?

'Greenwashing tricks us into believing change is happening, when in reality it's not'[12]

If a brand is claiming sustainability, don't take their word for it. Do your own research. You can check specific international brands at greenwash.com.[13]

I'll teach you where to look for information on garment and brand sustainability, how to read and assess garment tags, and how to identify fibre types and their impacts.

You can look at sustainability in three ways:

1. <u>Environmental:</u> This is the impact a brand or garment (including its supply chain, manufacture, use and/or disposal) has on the environment.

2. <u>Treatment of people:</u> This is the impact the fashion industry has on people, especially those making or dyeing garments – consider ethical sourcing.

3. <u>Treatment of animals:</u> This is a brand's or product's impact on animals – consider cruelty-free sourcing.

Navigating sustainability, ethics and fashion can feel overwhelming. Consumers can only do so much. The responsibility also belongs to the brands producing fashion and governments legislating it. My goal is to inspire you to ask as many questions as you can before buying, so your fashion choices are conscious ones. Don't feel like you need to do everything perfectly all at once; start with the parts that are most important to you and do your best with the resources you have.

No fashion company is perfect. To be honest, if we insisted on a perfect score before we purchased clothes, we'd all be naked.

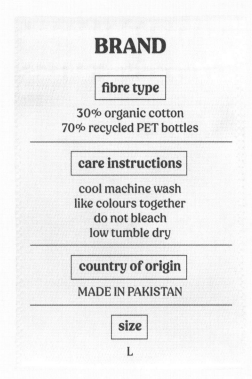

Where to start

Read the tag

To start gathering information on a garment's sustainability, read the tag. It will tell you an enormous amount about the garment.

Take note of these things:

- What is it made from? This includes fibres, threads, labels, trims and hardware (such as zips and buttons). (See Chapter 8: Know your fibre types, pages 62–72.)

- Are there detailed care instructions? (See Section 2: Care, pages 57–101.)

- Where was it made? (See 'Is it ethically made?', page 51.)

BRAND

fibre type

30% organic cotton
70% recycled PET bottles

care instructions

cool machine wash
like colours together
do not bleach
low tumble dry

country of origin

MADE IN PAKISTAN

size

L

Check the brand

What are the brand's policies? Look at the brand's website for information regarding their environmental impact, ethics and treatment of animals. Don't believe everything you read there – check other sources too.

What's the brand's reputation? Research broadly, outside of the brand's own website. Has anything been written about them in the media? Check greenwash.com or search the brand name plus 'sustainability' to find their sustainability policy (if they have one) as well as information from other sources.

What kind of packaging does the brand use to transport garments to you? Is it biodegradable or is everything wrapped in layers of plastic? Is the brand designing with circularity in mind? Does it offer free or cheap mending of its garments and take them back for recycling? Does it keep track of where its garments end up?

Are they transparent? A transparent brand publishes information on how workers are treated and whether they are paid a living wage; how garments are priced; and their environmental policies, practices and impacts. If the brand isn't being transparent, they may have something to hide.

Do they listen and respond to consumer feedback? Check their social media to see how they've responded to requests/criticism from consumers. Do they make positive changes when prompted?

If you can't find the information you're looking for, ask the brand directly and publicly. As consumers, we have the right to know exactly what we're buying and to demand brands be accountable, answer questions and improve. Remember, without consumers, brands can't exist. As a group, consumers hold power. If a significant number of consumers speak up, brands have to respond, or risk becoming irrelevant.

Check accreditations and certifications

Brands use certifications to make consumers feel like they are making an effort towards sustainability or ethics. Some certifications work well in certain aspects, but not many address the issues wholistically. It's important to remember that a certification or membership of a nice-sounding initiative is no guarantee of sustainability.[14] Many certifications have no independent oversight and lack accountability, transparency or independence. It is voluntary for brands to participate. This area of fashion desperately needs legislation and better governance. As usual, we as consumers should do our homework. Don't take certifications at face value as being a sign of sustainability or good ethics. Lobby brands, certifications and your government to do better.[15]

Good on You: Get the Good on You app or check their accompanying website for information on brands. Their rating system was developed in consultation with industry and organisations such as Fashion Revolution. Type in a brand name and you'll see a rating that ranges from 'We avoid' through to 'Great'. Their rating system is divided into three things they look at: planet, people and animals.[16]

GOTS: The Global Organic Textile Standard (GOTS) is a globally recognised and used textile certification. This standard applies ecological and social criteria to a product's entire textile supply chain, from raw material to end product, and decides whether it can be called organic. Brands apply for certification and are assessed independently. To become GOTS certified, they have to meet every criteria set by the standard.[17]

SA800: This certification doesn't apply to garments, only suppliers. Ask your brand if the factory producing your garment has this certification. It recognises business conducted in a way that is fair and decent for workers. It requires businesses to adhere to high social standards informed by the United Nations' Universal Declaration of Human Rights, the International Labour Organization's conventions and national laws.[18]

PETA: People for the Ethical Treatment of Animals (PETA) believe that animals do not exist for humans to experiment on, eat, wear, use for entertainment or abuse in any other way. A PETA-approved logo on a tag means the brand or specific product has met a set of criteria determined by PETA. They state that their 'Cruelty-Free' logo means a product is not tested on animals and/or is vegan (i.e. does not include any animal products).[19]

B CORP: B Corp certification was developed by the not-for-profit organisation B Lab, which is working to improve environmental and ethical standards in business. B Corp certification means that a business has met a series of standards in social and environmental performance, is accountable to all stakeholders, and exhibits transparency. While B Corp certification may not be listed on the tag, it's something you can check for on a brand's website.[20]

OEKO-TEX®: The OEKO-TEX® organisation consists of independent textile- and leather-testing institutes in Europe and Japan. It offers different levels of certifications based on the verification of a product's safety and production processes for health and the environment. Look for this certification on clothing tags or company websites.[21]

For a comprehensive analysis and comparison of certifications and their effectiveness, look at the Changing Markets Foundation report: *License to greenwash.*

Does the brand contribute to initiatives in a committed way?

Does the brand donate money, time or promotion to initiatives that make the world a better place? Note that jumping on the bandwagon of a trending cause for a one-off contribution isn't the same as committing to ongoing donations to a worthy cause.

Where was it made and why?

When we think about where something is made, we should consider whether it has travelled around the world to get to us, and ask why it's being made in a particular place.

Carbon footprint

A product's carbon footprint refers to the amount of greenhouse gas produced to create and transport the product. You can calculate your fashion carbon footprint using an online calculator created by ThredUp.[22]

A garment's carbon footprint doesn't begin when a piece of clothing is made; it includes the journey from raw material until it reaches you and beyond. The carbon footprint of a product is added to throughout the supply chain, manufacturing process, transport and disposal, including:

- **farming or creation of the raw materials used to construct the textile**
- **transport to where it is milled and woven**
- **energy needed to process and weave the fibre**
- **transport to the place where it is manufactured into a garment**
- **energy required to manufacture**
- **transport to the place where it is sold**
- **energy required to run that store or warehouse**
- **transport to the consumer**
- **energy required to recycle or dispose of it.**

Each step of this supply chain uses fossil fuels, creating carbon. If fabric is grown in the same place it's milled, woven, made into garments and sold, much less carbon is generated. This is why buying local is better, but it's not always possible and this kind of system is pretty rare in fashion.

Is it ethically made?

When you check the tag to see where a garment has been made, find out whether the country of manufacture is regulated by laws that protect garment and textile workers and the local environment.

Brands have garments produced offshore for reasons including:

- **lower wage costs for workers**[23]

- **lack of industry regulation (i.e. environmental and human rights laws either don't exist or are poorly policed)**

- **weak or non-existent labour unions (meaning workers don't have representation, aren't protected and can't strike for better pay or conditions).**

Garment workers are entitled to safe, dignified working conditions, a living wage and equal working rights, so check whether the brands you choose to support are doing the right thing. The real burden of brands not doing the right thing is carried by those who can least afford it: the garment workers, often women.[24]

Here's how to find out if a garment is ethical:

- **View the brand's website to check if they are transparent about their policies around ethics and sustainability.**

- **Research the brand widely to see if their practices have been reported elsewhere.**

- **Check their rating on Good on You.**

- **Look at the Fashion Revolution website and their most recent Fashion Transparency Index Report to see if the brand is listed.**[25]

- **Look for B Corp, OEKO-TEX®, Fair Trade, GOTS, FSC (Forest Stewardship Council) and Woolmark certifications, as these accreditations address ethical as well as environmental concerns.**

- **See whether the country of origin is listed on the Global Slavery Index (GSI). Textile workers from these countries are at risk of modern slavery.**[26]

- **Check whether they are accredited by Ethical Clothing Australia.**

You can get more information on fashion and ethics from:

- **Fashion Revolution**
- **Clean Clothes Campaign**
- **Good on You**
- **Walkfree.org**
- **Ellen McArthur Foundation**
- **Ethical Clothing Australia.**

CHAPTER 7: COULD YOU LEARN TO MAKE IT YOURSELF?

When I'm looking for clothes, I can never find what I want in the shops. I know it's odd for a lover of clothes and fabric, but I can honestly admit that I intensely dislike clothes shopping. It makes me feel self-conscious and irritated; nothing ever fits perfectly and I feel claustrophobic in fitting rooms. I can also be pretty critical when it comes to fabric types and stitching quality. Second-hand shopping is the exception – I love with all my heart the potential of finding a vintage treasure.

Being unable to find what I wanted in the shops was one of the main reasons I started making my own clothes. I make the clothes I want to see in stores. This is the only way I've found to combine the shapes I want to wear with fabrics I love, in sizes that actually fit. These days, my style philosophy is to stick to what I know suits my body shape and makes me feel great, then make it in every colour. To this, I add special vintage pieces.

Learning to sew takes a little time and effort, but can free you from relying on what big brands present to you as the latest trend. You can control what your clothes are made from, and nothing will give you a greater sense of accomplishment than loving yourself sick in an outfit entirely made by you, knowing you're reducing packaging, waste and your carbon footprint.

If you're looking for a sewing machine, buy an old one that's been well looked after. Give it some oil, change the needles, read the manual and have it serviced. When they're maintained properly, sewing machines can last forever and owning one gives you more options in the kinds of repairs you can do.

How to learn

- **Learn some of the basics in Section 3: Keep (pages 103–198).**

- **You'll find a YouTube video for every technique, and patterns available online for every style you can think of.**

- **Lots of community schools and small businesses offer beginner sewing courses. Joining a class means you get to meet other stitchers in your local area.**

- **Start a sewing group to share fabrics, skills, sewing machines and patterns.**

- **Ask someone in your family to teach you a skill if they know how to sew, embroider, knit or crochet. They may have been busting to be asked and it's great to pass down these skills through generations.**

The golden rules of fabric shopping

1. Use fabric you already own or fabric from another garment you own and want to transform.

2. Source biodegradable second-hand fabric. Keep in mind that second-hand synthetic fabrics will continue to release microplastics when they are washed and disposed of.

3. Swap or trade for second-hand fabrics.

4. Look for deadstock fabrics. These are excess fabrics from designers or manufacturers.

5. If you're buying new, source local, sustainable and ethically made if possible.

6. If local fabric isn't an option, choose recycled cotton or wool, or organic hemp or linen fabric first.

7. If none of the above are available, your last choice should be the fast-fashion equivalents of the fabric world. Before you buy, ask fabric retailers what their fabrics are made of, where they were made, who made them and what their working conditions were like. If they are unable to answer these questions, be wary.

8. Whether it's new or second-hand, follow the 'Know your fibre type' guidelines in Chapter 8 (see pages 62–72) when sourcing fabric. Stay away from cheap polyesters and synthetics – they're not only polluting but are tricky to sew with. Don't forget that mono-fabrics are easier to recycle than fibre blends, so look for 100% of a single fibre type.

This list also applies to threads, zips, trims, linings, interfacings, elastic and anything else you add to a garment during its construction. Think about what these are made from and their impacts. Adding a polyester trim makes a garment harder to recycle. Polyester sewing threads also need to be removed before recycling or composting a garment made from natural fibres.

Support local patternmakers if you can, and if you're downloading patterns from the internet, make sure their creators have been paid fairly.

A NOTE ON JOINING FABRIC PIECES

Most of the projects in this book call for fabric scraps and offer upcycling recommendations. If your fabric scraps aren't big enough to make your desired project, cut the edges of the fabric pieces as straight as possible, then patch them together, building up the size of your fabric bit by bit. I use a flat-felled seam for joining fabrics so the fabric is reversible. To do this:

1. Sew the right-hand sides of two pieces of fabric together with a 1.5 cm (½ inch) seam allowance.

2. Press the seam open.

3. Trim 1 cm (⅓ inch) from one seam allowance.

4. Press both seams to the left.

5. Fold the longer seam over the shorter one and iron it.

6. Press all seams to the right and edge-stitch 2 mm (⅛ inch) from the folded edge.

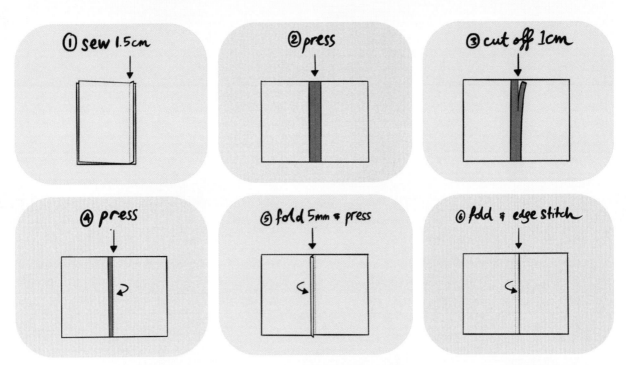

① sew 1.5cm

② press

③ cut off 1cm

④ press

⑤ fold 5mm & press

⑥ fold & edge stitch

SECTION 2

CARE

I own the most beautiful 1950s black, fluffy wool jacket. It belonged to my friend Koji's grandmother, who wore it over her kimono in Kyoto winters. It has secret pockets and space in the sleeves for kimono sleeves to sit inside perfectly. I love this jacket and care for it religiously. I brush it, air it out and mend the beautiful, green silk lining when it needs help. I look forward to the cold months just so I can wear it, because it's like wearing a warm, fuzzy, stylish cocoon. I always feel great in it.

In the nearly 20 years I've owned it, I've never washed it or had it dry-cleaned. If it gets dirty, I spot-clean that area. If it starts to smell musty, I hang it outside in the breeze on a sunny day. When I'm storing it for winter, I put chunks of camphor laurel wood in the pockets to keep moths away. I fully intend to own this jacket until the end of my life, and I know it will last the distance because of my care. It's lasted nearly 75 years already and there's no reason it can't last another 75.

'Care for your clothes, like the good friends they are.' — Joan Crawford

The best way to make clothes last is to care for them. We can do this by taking the time to understand them, making sure we know what they're made from and learning how to care for that particular fibre type. Care is an important part of seeing our clothes as valuable treasures, which we've collected for a reason, rather than as disposable and replaceable.

We're seeing huge environmental issues arise from the waste, carbon emissions and pollution created by the fashion industry. The world can't sustain the production of clothes at current volumes, nor the staggering amount being thrown away. Things need to change, and caring for the clothes we already own is a good place to start. If we can extend the life of each garment indefinitely, we reduce the need to replace them and thereby keep them out of landfill.

Cleaning clothes has an impact on the environment because it requires energy, water and chemicals. We can reduce this impact by being conscious of how often we wash, the temperatures we wash at, and how much water and detergent we use. Reducing how often we dry-clean and use the dryer can also reduce our impact significantly.

Have a think about what you're able to care for before you buy. If you don't realistically have time for handwashing or following care instructions, that's no bother. Look for hardy natural fibres rather than 'handwash only' silk or wool garments. That being said, it's not hard to learn how to care for even the finest silk.

If you're willing to learn (and take a little bit of extra time sorting your loads), nothing will feel too intimidating to care for and your clothes will last a lot longer.

This section will show you how to care for each fibre type, interpret care instructions, wash less and minimise your impact while caring for clothes.

8 steps of care for long-lasting clothing

1. Read the label:

a) Follow care instructions (see pages 81–83).

b) Know what it's made from and how to care for that particular fibre (see pages 62–72 and 89–93).

2. Wash only when it's absolutely necessary (see pages 75–88).

3. Separate colours.

4. Wash to minimise impact – one washing cycle does not suit all garments.

5. Maintain clothes between wears.

6. Keep clothes safe from damp and insects.

7. Minimise using the clothes dryer.

8. Minimise dry-cleaning.

CHAPTER 8: KNOW YOUR FIBRE TYPES

I had so many questions. The patchy stories that accompanied the suitcase were fascinating. Some clothes had been passed down from my great-grandmother; others were collected during my grandmother's childhood in Thailand. Looking at the petticoats and camisoles, I imagined my great-grandmother and her mother dressing in the many layers of the time, and couldn't believe how lucky I was to see and touch clothes that they'd worn and cared for.

This suitcase held the story of my family as well as stories of other families, travel and dispossession. I need to delve into the political and social histories of Thailand, China and Australia to find out why these magnificent robes have ended up here with me. I've tried to decode the symbols on the robes and date them. I haven't even scratched the surface of this yet. I could spend years figuring out the contents of this suitcase – I wish I had more time to do it!

My grandmother once gave me a suitcase of treasure. It didn't smell great because it had been sitting in her humid garage in Sydney for years. When I opened it, I couldn't believe my eyes. It was full of incredible antique clothing: Edwardian petticoats with handmade lace trims, tiny leather gloves and beautiful frilly bloomers mixed in with some jaw-dropping embroidered Chinese silk robes and shoes.

All this is to say that fabric is important to us. Since humans started wearing cloth, painting, dyeing, embroidering and making patterns on cloth have been used to tell human stories and pass them down through generations. The fabrics we wear today also hold the stories of the places their raw materials were grown, and their spinners, weavers and designers. The fabrics you wear hold part of your story. When we repair or embellish our fabrics, and look after them so they last, we turn them into items with the potential to be passed down to our own great-grandchildren. What will the fabrics you're wearing now say about you?

Responsible fabric choice

Fabric spends more time sitting close to our bodies than pretty much anything else. We breathe in its fibres and our skin absorbs whatever it's been dyed or treated with. For a product that looms so large in most of our lives (unless you're a naturist), it follows that we should be curious about what our clothes are made from. We should be thoughtful about our fabric choices, ask lots of questions about where and how the fabrics were made, and care where they end up. We should be thinking of fabric as an important, long-term choice.

Fabric impacts people and the environment for its entire life cycle

The processes used to create each fabric type impact the people who make the fabrics and places they're made. The way we wash and care for fabrics once they've been made into clothes continues to impact us, other people and the environment. Fabric affects our bodies when we wear it. Even when fabric has been disposed of, it continues to have impact. So fabric choice isn't simple. Every fabric type has its advantages and disadvantages. Not all natural fibres are sustainable and not all synthetic fibres are unsustainable. This section will help guide you through the pros and cons of different fabrics.

Synthetic fibres

- Polyester
- Nylon (polyamide)
- Spandex/elastane (polyurethane)
- Acrylic (acrylonitrile)
- Olefin (polyethylene, polypropylene)
- Aramids
- PVC/vinyl

'In the midst of a climate emergency, the number one raw material for textile fibre is oil and gas.'[31]

Polyester

Polyester is the synthetic fibre used in polyester fabric. Right now, it's the most widely produced fabric in the world. It's easy to wash, doesn't need ironing, is cheap and easy for manufacturers to produce, and mostly uses less water and land to produce than natural fibres.[27]

So what's the problem with it? Well, the bad news is that polyester and other synthetic fibres are made from plastic, which is derived from non-renewable petroleum produced by the fossil fuel industry.[28] Not only is the fossil fuel industry a big polluter, but the process of manufacturing and dyeing polyester is chemical heavy, energy intensive and greenhouse gas emitting.[29] The fabric itself continues to pollute by shedding plastic microfibres throughout its life cycle, even after it's been disposed of or recycled. Synthetic fabrics are not biodegradable.[30]

Fossil fuels are a finite, polluting resource and synthetic fibre production relies on this resource. We simply can't keep extracting and using fossil fuels at our current pace; first, because their extraction and use cause harm, and second, because they will eventually run out. With cleaner production, improved recycling technology and closed loops, we should never need to produce it as a virgin raw material.

What are microfibres?

All fabrics shed microfibres when we wear them, wash them and dispose of them. Synthetic fabrics shed plastic microfibres called microplastics, which end up in our oceans and in fish, animals, our food and us![32] It takes hundreds of years for them to break down in the environment. As they break down, they can cause damage to the organisms and ecosystems around them by attracting other pollutants such as chemical contaminants and heavy metals.[33] Plastic particles from synthetic materials may be contributing up to 35% of the primary plastic polluting our oceans.[34] Every time we wash a synthetic garment, up to 1900 individual plastic fibres can be rinsed off and released into wastewater treatment plants that cannot filter them.[35]

'Microfibres are so tiny they can easily move through sewage treatment plants. They do not biodegrade and bind with molecules from harmful chemicals found in wastewater. They are then eaten by small fishes and plankton, concentrating toxins and going up the food chain until they reach us. The consequences of microfibres on the human body have yet to be researched and revealed.'[36]

'Consumers interact with the material qualities of polyester daily, but rarely do we think of ourselves as wearing plastic.'[37]

Other synthetic fabrics, such as acrylic, nylon and elastane, also shed plastic microfibres. And a mix of natural and synthetic fibres will still shed plastic fibres.

Activewear

That stretch in your activewear likely comes from plastic such as spandex or elastane. These materials are made from petrochemicals that may also be formulated with harmful chemical additives like phthalates and bisphenols. *The Guardian* newspaper has reported on new evidence suggesting that oily substances in our sweat 'help the bad chemicals to come out of the microplastic fibres and become available for human absorption'.[38] In other words, as we exercise, our bodies may be absorbing chemicals that can cause cancer and disrupt hormones. Along with the other issues associated with these fabrics, this puts activewear at the top of the 'least sustainable' list.

Best choice synthetic fibres

My advice with polyester and synthetic fibres is to avoid buying them until the industry improves on sustainable production, waste management, circularity and recycling. Great advances are being made in this area with exciting innovations being explored. The day when we can recycle garments and fibres without using water or chemicals, with very little energy and without creating more waste is coming closer. More work needs to be done; while the fashion industry is slow to respond, change is happening.

Synthetic fabrics come in varying degrees of quality. Some higher-quality fabrics last well, look good after washing, are recyclable and shed fewer microplastics than cheaply produced synthetics. Because synthetic fabrics don't have a widely recognised sustainability rating system, it can be hard to gauge quality. One way is to check whether the brand is committed to sustainable practices, such as the use of mono-fibres (single fibre types), zero-waste clothing production and designing for circularity, and is transparent about its use of and responsibility for synthetics.

Clothing made from recycled plastic bottles is not sustainable or a smart use of materials. This is an example of downcycling, in which an infinitely recyclable product (a PET plastic bottle) is taken out of the loop and turned into a low-quality, microplastic-polluting product (synthetic clothing), which can't be turned back into a bottle and is statistically likely to end up in landfill.[39]

The best choice for synthetic fabrics are to buy them second-hand. Then look for mechanically recycled polyester and nylon. Next, choose chemically recycled polyester and nylon. Your last choice should be polyacrylic, virgin polyester, PET and spandex. Look for mono-materials, or fabrics made from a single fibre type such as 100% polyester, because these are easier to recycle than fabrics made from a blend of fibres.[40]

If you already own polyester clothing, don't throw it out. Check 'How to wash according to fibre type: Polyester and synthetics' (page 89) to find out how to minimise its impact. If you're at a clothing swap and spot something great made of polyester, think about its ongoing environmental effects before you choose it.

Regenerated (semi-synthetic) fibres

- Acetate
- Bamboo rayon
- Cupro
- Lyocell
- Milk casein
- Modal
- Ramie
- Rayon
- Soybean protein
- Tencel
- Viscose

These fabrics are derived from natural resources, but go through an intensive chemical transformation process, leaving no trace of the original plant.[41] Some are made from cellulose, one of the basic building blocks of plant cells. Cellulose fabrics can come from materials such as straw, cotton waste or wood pulp. Some come from protein fibres such as soybeans and milk.

They are marketed as natural fibres *but* are heavily processed and a long way away from their original plant matter. Some are biodegradable, but chemical modifications used during production can prevent biodegradation.

'The truth is, most "bamboo" textile products, if not all, really are rayon, which typically is made using environmentally toxic chemicals in a process that emits hazardous pollutants into the air. Although different plants, including bamboo, can be used as a source material to create rayon, there's no trace of the original plant in the finished rayon product.'[42]

Some of the drawbacks of these fabrics are:

- They come from trees or plants. Trees need to be cut down, so forests are being cleared to produce fabrics. So if you do buy cellulose-based fabrics, make sure they are FSC or PEFC (Programme for the Endorsement of Forest Certification) certified, meaning they come from a sustainably managed forest or plantation.[43]

- Converting a tree into fabric needs a lot of energy. This process relies heavily on chemicals, which can cause pollution that harms people and the environment.[44]

- Some companies are more responsible than others. Like with synthetic fibres, innovative work is being done to reduce the impact of manufacturing these fabrics. Increasingly, companies are being transparent with consumers about their processes, working to eliminate the discharge of hazardous solvents and chemicals during the manufacturing process, sourcing their raw materials from sustainably managed forests, and making sure their products are compostable and biodegradable. Unfortunately, this is not always the case, so seek out brands that are doing the right thing.[45]

Best choice regenerated (semi-synthetic) fibres

Second-hand fabrics or garments are the best choice here, because they don't shed microplastics and will last a long time when they're good quality. Next, look for Tencel brand Lyocell, Crailar flax or Monocel Bamboo; then Ramie and modal. Bamboo viscose, viscose and rayon should be your last choice. These fabrics are mostly biodegradable as long as they haven't been treated with chemicals during processing.[46]

Natural plant fibres

- Coir
- Cotton
- Hemp
- Jute
- Kapok
- Linen (flax)
- Sisal

Natural plant fibres come from different plant species, such as cotton from the cotton plant, or linen from the flax plant. In their raw forms, they're biodegradable.

Hemp and linen

Fibres such as hemp and linen are among the most sustainable because they grow quickly and don't require a lot of water or chemicals to produce. If you can find these fabrics in organic form, they're the most sustainable choice you can make overall in terms of fabrics.[47]

Cotton

Natural fibres aren't without their issues. Don't be fooled: natural doesn't always mean sustainable. Cotton is the bad boy on this list; the plants require huge amounts of water, land and chemicals to farm and process. Cotton fibres are bleached and dyed as part of their processing, sometimes using harmful chemicals. Cotton farms have a long history of unethical farming practices and poor treatment of workers, and cotton continues to be harvested by men, women and children working in conditions akin to modern slavery.[48] So yes, cotton is biodegradable, but in sustainability terms, it's sometimes on par with synthetic fibres.

Best choice natural plant fibres

As always, look for second-hand first. The next best choice is recycled cotton, hemp or linen. Organic linen and organic hemp are the absolute best choice in terms of new natural plant fibres, and the best fabric choices overall. This is followed by organic cotton and conventional linen or hemp. Try to find them unblended with synthetic fibres so they are easier to recycle. Look for certifications on labels such as OEKO-TEX® and GOTS.

Natural animal fibres

- Alpaca
- Angora
- Camel hair
- Cashmere
- Horsehair
- Llama
- Mohair
- Silk
- Wool
- Yak

Natural fibres that come from animals are biodegradable in their pure forms, but can vary greatly in how the animals were treated. It's a good idea to look into certifications for each product or brand. PETA has a certification system for the treatment of animals.

Wool

Certain breeds of sheep (such as Merino) are bred for the purpose of growing wool. They are shorn regularly and their fleeces are washed and spun into threads that are then woven or knitted into fabrics or left as yarn. Wool is breathable, recyclable, biodegradable and has excellent durability if treated with care. Unlike polyester or acrylic fibres, wool doesn't shed polluting microplastics and doesn't need washing as frequently as other fibre types, saving water and energy.[49]

The downside is that wool relies on sheep farming, which takes a heavy environmental toll. Livestock farming creates methane, a harmful greenhouse gas, and requires land clearing for grazing, contributing to biodiversity loss and erosion. Scouring wool to prepare it for processing requires chemicals and water. Farming sheep for wool is associated with animal cruelty concerns. In Australia, sheep go through painful processes including mulesing, tail-docking and castration without anaesthetic, and can be injured in the shearing process.[50] To find mulesing-free wool, check whether your brand adheres to the National Wool Declaration or look for the Responsible Wool Standard (RWS) label.[51]

Some exciting improvements are being made in the wool industry, with organisations like Fibershed in the USA creating the Regional Fiber Manufacturing Initiative and Climate Beneficial™ Wool. This organisation supports local producers in producing cleaner and safer wool, aiming for a net-positive system where wool production can create carbon credits and improve the local environment.[52]

Silk

Strong, light, warm and absorbent, silk is a gorgeous fabric to wear. It drapes beautifully, takes dye unlike any other fabric and has a magical lustre. Silk is biodegradable in its raw form but, unfortunately, it also has its downsides.

Silk is spun by silkworms, specifically mulberry leaf–munching caterpillars mostly of the *Bombyx mori* species. The caterpillars spin a cocoon to protect themselves during their metamorphosis into moths. This cocoon is used to make silk fabric; it is boiled, unwound into a long continuous filament and spun into threads, which are then woven or knitted into fabric.

During silk-making, the chrysalis is usually killed using hot air or steam so it doesn't break through the cocoon, keeping the silk filament long and unbroken.[53]

Silk is associated with insect cruelty concerns. Silk extraction is labour intensive and uses a lot of water, energy and sometimes harmful chemicals. It can be tricky to get trustworthy and accurate information about labour practices in this industry.[54]

Peace or ahimsa silk is often spoken about as an alternative to conventional silk. Here, the silkworm is allowed to break out of the cocoon before it is boiled. However, it's not always a case of a happy moth flying free to complete its life cycle. After centuries being bred for silk production, these insects often can't live long beyond the cocoon stage, and aren't able to survive in the wild.[55]

Cashmere, alpaca, mohair, angora

These materials all come from the hair of animals. They are beautiful fabrics to wear that are biodegradable in their raw forms. They have similar sustainability disadvantages to wool in that their production requires a lot of land, labour, energy and resources, and they have been associated with animal cruelty.

Leather and fur

Leather comes from the skin of an animal. Fur is both the skin and fur of an animal. Leather and fur come from many different animals, including cows, sheep, pigs, rabbits, kangaroos, crocodiles and snakes. All leather is treated (or tanned) with chemicals to stop it from breaking down.

Leather and fur are associated with a suite of sustainability, animal and human rights issues. Leather is a by-product of the meat industry, which produces huge amounts of greenhouse gases, requires cleared land for grazing and the eventual death of an animal. This industry still has a lot of work to do to address these issues. Some farms and businesses are making great progress towards sustainability and animal welfare, so support these businesses when you can.

Look out for the exciting new developments happening in natural leather alternatives, with items made from pineapple, kombucha and algae. But steer clear of 'vegan leather' made from PVC because it's just plastic.

Best choice natural animal fibres

While it may be possible to improve the carbon footprint of silk with more efficient farming practices, the best practice is to try to find silk second-hand if you can. When it has been properly cared for, silk can last forever and will stay beautifully lustrous. Look for organic silk first, but check labour practices. Peace silk and wild silk can also be sourced, but labour practices may still be an issue. Before you buy new silk, ask brands about where and how they source their silk to see how transparent they are.[56]

Buying second-hand or recycled wool, cashmere, alpaca, mohair and angora is an excellent choice because garments made from these fibres last well, are easy and fun to repair, and are biodegradable or recyclable at the end of their useful lives. Wool is lovely to wear, keeping you warm in winter and cool in summer. Look for 100% of one fibre type rather than a blend because this is easier to recycle.

With any natural animal-fibre fabric or garment, do your research carefully and demand brands provide information relating to animal treatment, labour practices and the sustainability of their production practices.

Consumer power

Fashion designers, manufacturers and brands have a responsibility to create sustainable garments ethically, track the life cycle of their garments, offer free or affordable repairs, and accept items back for re-manufacture at the end of their wearable life. Choose not to purchase from brands who don't do this.

Governments, too, have a responsibility to legislate for ethics and sustainability, and hold producers to account. As consumers, we can apply pressure to industry to comply with these responsibilities through the choices we make, but we also need to ensure our voices are heard, telling companies and governments to do the right thing. You can use social media to bring attention to these issues, and send emails to your local member of parliament demanding change. Use your voice to promote companies and parliamentarians who you see doing the right thing.

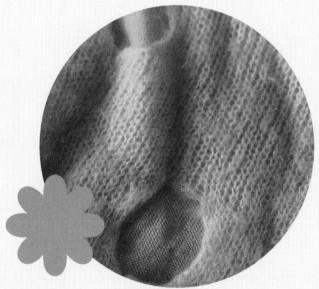

CHAPTER 9: BEFORE YOU WASH

I encourage you to stop and think before throwing things into the wash. I get it – we're all busy and washing is boring. But taking a minute to consider what you're washing and how you're washing it can prevent shrinkage, colour-bleed, fading, pills and warping. These are all reasons why clothes end up in the bin. All this washing is ageing our clothes prematurely. So before you wash, read on.

Read the label

The first thing to look at when you're buying or caring for clothes is the label. The label usually includes all the information you need to clean that garment correctly, as well as other important information such as where it was made, what it's made from and the size. Sometimes, you even get a spare button and the right colour thread to sew it on with!

If the fibre type is listed but the care label isn't specific about how to care for it, this chapter has instructions on how to care for each fibre type. If I haven't listed it here, search 'how to care for [fibre type]'. Read a couple of articles and compare the advice to see if they agree. Keep digging until you find a few advising the same method and use that one.

It's important to follow the care instructions on labels. The label lists the most conservative ways to care for that garment. If you're a pro at caring for garments, you'll know when to disregard a 'dry-clean only' label for wool and silk items that you're confident handwashing; otherwise, ignore care labels at your own risk.

Air it out

Does it really need a wash?

I'm about to make your life a whole lot easier – we wash our clothes too often. Levi's recommends its customers to wash their jeans after 10 wears! Wool items probably only need to be washed at the end of each season.

Ask yourself before you wash: is it really dirty or are you washing it out of habit? Try stretching out the time between washes. Each load you save reduces your power, water and detergent use, and prolongs the life of your clothes. Here are some ways to keep your clothes smelling great, looking clean and lasting longer … without washing after every wear.[57]

Air it out

If you're worried your garment is getting smelly between washes, turn it inside out and hang it in the sun. The heat, light and fresh air will get rid of musty smells and bacteria. For non-colourfast or naturally dyed garments, air them out in the shade.

Steam it

If you have a steamer, you can use it to freshen clothes. The steam's heat kills bacteria and –added bonus – your clothes will also be wrinkle free! If your iron has a steam function, use it in the same way. Just hang your garment on a coat hanger, hold the iron at least 5 cm (2 inches) away from the garment if synthetic, and shoot steam through the fabric.

Steam it

Spot-cleaning and 'spritzing'

If your garment is clean aside from a small patch, spot-cleaning saves you time and water (see the Spot-cleaning technique on page 79). A bacteria-killing spritz (see recipe on page 77) can also keep your clothes smelling great between washes. We use it in on costumes in the film industry when there isn't time to wash them between wears.

'SPRITZ' RECIPE

|||||||||||||||||||||||||||||||||||||||||||||||||

Try to reuse an empty spray bottle for this rather than buying a new one. If you have a spray bottle from a cleaning product (not bleach-based) just give it a good rinse first. Glass is better than plastic because you'll be able to keep and refill your spritz bottle indefinitely. The measurements for this recipe don't need to be exact, but the ratio should be about one-third vodka to two-thirds water and a few drops of eucalyptus essential oil. Try to find vodka with minimal additives.

Difficulty rating:
Easy

Time needed:
10 minutes

What you'll need

500 ml (17 oz) spray bottle

100 ml (3.5 oz) vodka

300 ml (10 oz) water

5 drops eucalyptus or lemon essential oil

NOTE: Test this spritz on an inconspicuous area of your garment before using it on anything delicate. Essential oils can sometimes leave stains on delicate fabrics. This spritz is great for refreshing winter coats before putting them away for summer because the essential oil will also help to keep moths away. Make sure everything is absolutely dry before you pack it away.

1. Hang the garment on a coat hanger inside out, outdoors if possible. Hold the spray bottle 20 cm (8 inches) away from the garment and mist the spritz over it. Concentrate more on sweaty areas like the underarms and crotch. Try not to saturate the garment, just make it slightly damp.

2. Let the garment dry out in the sun and breeze, and make sure it's properly dry before returning it to your wardrobe.

SPOT-CLEANING TECHNIQUE

I use this technique if I'm in a hurry – if I'm dressed and ready to go out, only to discover a stain on the front of my shirt. I often do it while I'm still wearing the garment. I'll remove the stain, dry the wet patch with a hairdryer and run out the door!

Difficulty rating:
Easy

Time needed:
5 minutes

NOTE: If your garment is a delicate fabric, use the appropriate detergent for that fabric (e.g. woolwash for a wool garment). Gentle eco dishwashing liquid will work well on most fabrics and is especially good for oil stains.

What you'll need

2 light-coloured wash cloths or absorbent fabric scraps

Eco dishwashing liquid

Water

1. Keep one cloth dry and hold it inside the garment at the back of the stain. Wet the other cloth slightly. Squeeze a tiny amount of eco dishwashing liquid onto the stain and scratch it gently with your fingernail then use your damp cloth to gently blot the detergent through the fabric onto the cloth underneath. The inside cloth should soak up the stain and water as you go.

2. Repeat this process until the stain is gone, blotting through the fabric. Use more water on the damp cloth if you need to. If it's a big stain and the inside cloth gets dirty or very wet, replace it with another clean, dry cloth so you're not spreading dirt around.

3. Hang the garment outside to dry, or dry the patch using the cool setting on a hairdryer if you're in a hurry.

CHAPTER 10: WHEN IT REALLY NEEDS A WASH

When a wash becomes inevitable, don't forget to check care labels first and follow those instructions. Then follow this list:

1. Treat stains first.

2. Unbutton buttons, unroll sleeves and check pockets.

3. Separate colours.

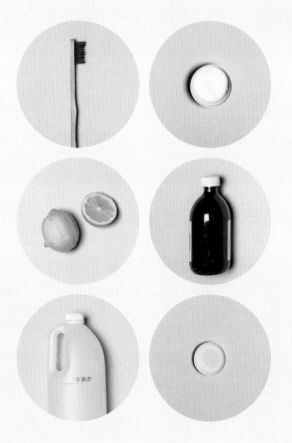

Stain removal

The trick with stains is to get to them quickly – the sooner you treat the stain, the easier it will be to remove. Before using any stain-removing product, including a homemade one, test it on an inconspicuous area of the garment first to make sure it doesn't affect the colour or damage the fabric.

What to keep in your stain-removing kit:

- Old toothbrush (for gentle agitation of stains)

- Bicarbonate of soda/baking soda (gets rid of smells, good as a pre-soak to remove stains)

- Lemon juice (a natural bleach and a great stain or rust remover on clothes)

- Hydrogen peroxide 3% solution (a mild oxygenating bleach, safer than chlorine bleach – spot-check first)

- White cleaning vinegar (brings shine and softness back to silk and wool after washing, also a natural stain and mould remover)

- Eco dishwashing liquid (dissolves oil and grease stains)

Separate colours

Unfortunately, we can't assume that one wash cycle will work for all of our clothes, so before you wash, take a minute to check labels and separate colours, even if you're handwashing. This can save colour-bleed disasters and will keep your blacks looking black and whites bright for longer. I sometimes even separate cool tones (blues and greens) from warm tones (reds and yellows) to prevent colours from blending with each other in the wash.

Interpretation of care labels

Care labels often include symbols, which aren't always accompanied by text explaining what they mean. There are six basic symbols on care labels. Each one relates to a different aspect of garment care. Dots or lines added to the symbols tell you about things like temperature limits or restrictions.

- Triangles = bleaching instructions
- Tubs with water = washing
- Squares = drying
- Twists of fabric = wringing
- Circles = dry-cleaning
- Irons = ironing

A cross through any of these symbols means *don't do it*. Here's the full list of symbols:[58]

INTERPRETATION OF CARE LABELS

Bleaching		Washing		Drying	
△	Any type of bleach can be used	🤚 (in washtub)	Hand wash only	**Air drying**	
		(washtub)	Machine wash okay	(line in box) Air dry on the line	
		(washtub)	Low spin speed	(lines in box) Drip dry	
△ (striped)	Non-chlorine or oxygenated bleach okay to use	(washtub, one line)	Gentle wash (can be spun/rinsed)	(line in box) Dry flat	
		(washtub crossed)	Do not wash	**Electric dryer**	
		(washtub 30°)	Max wash temp 30°	(circle, one dot) Dry on low heat	
△ (crossed)	Do not bleach (Never use bleach on wool, silk or leather)	(washtub one dot)	Cold wash only	(circle, two dots) Dry on medium heat	
		(washtub two dots)	Warm wash okay	(circle, three dots) Dry on high heat	
		(washtub three dots)	Hot wash okay	(circle in square) Tumble dry	
				(circle in square crossed) Not suitable for a clothes dryer	

Wringing		Dry-cleaning		Ironing	
	Okay to wring out by hand	○	Okay to dry clean		Okay to iron at any temp
		P	These symbols tell dry cleaners what method and chemicals to use		Only iron on low temp (wool, silk, delicates)
		A			Iron on medium temp or lower (synthetics)
	Do not wring out by hand	F			Okay to iron on high temp (linen and cotton)
		⊗	Do not dry clean		
					Do not use steam
		Short cycle			
		Low heat			Do not iron

COTTON STAIN REMOVER RECIPE

|||||||||||||||||||||||||||||||||||||||||||||||||||||||||||||||||||||||||||||||||||||

This stain remover is great for removing ink and wine stains. Use it on light-coloured cotton clothes, testing it on an inconspicuous part of the garment before applying it anywhere noticeable. Don't use hydrogen peroxide on silk or wool. You can find hydrogen peroxide 3% solution at the chemist.

Difficulty rating:
Easy

Time needed:
10 minutes

What you'll need

2 tablespoons (6 teaspoons) hydrogen peroxide 3% solution

1 tablespoon (3 teaspoons) eco dishwashing liquid

Kitchen gloves

Light-coloured towel

1 teaspoon bicarbonate of soda/baking soda (optional)

1. Mix the hydrogen peroxide and dishwashing liquid together. Wear kitchen gloves to avoid getting hydrogen peroxide on your hands and don't get it in your eyes.

2. Place the towel underneath the garment you're treating. You can even put the towel inside the garment to soak up any excess liquid.

3. Spread the stain remover onto the stained area. Gently rub the liquid into the stain with the old toothbrush from your stain-removal kit. Let it sit on the stain for at least 1 hour before rinsing and washing as normal.

4. If the stain is particularly well set in, sprinkle 1 teaspoon bicarbonate of soda onto the stain before adding the peroxide mixture.

YELLOW STAINS AND ODOUR REMOVER RECIPE

Care Project

||||||||||||||||||||||||||||||||||||||||||||||

This remover is great for getting rid of body odour under the arms or yellow rings around the underarms and neck. Test this paste on an inconspicuous area of the garment first.

Difficulty rating:
Easy

Time needed:
10 minutes

What you'll need

2 tablespoons (6 teaspoons) bicarbonate of soda/baking soda

1 tablespoon (3 teaspoons) lemon juice

1. Mix the bicarbonate of soda and lemon juice in a bowl. Apply the mixture to the underarms and collar of your garment with an old toothbrush or a spoon and leave it to sit for at least a couple of hours, ideally overnight.

2. The next morning, rinse it off and wash it as usual. Hanging the garment in the sun to dry will help to get rid of any yellow staining.

Wash to minimise impact

The right detergent

It's important to think about what's in the detergent we use. Choosing the right one can be very confusing, so let me help you navigate your way through the cleaning aisle.

Ingredients

Don't assume ingredients are safe just because they are being used in detergent. Some synthetic chemical compounds used in detergents have been linked to cancer; they can be toxic for people washing and wearing clothes washed in these detergents, as well as for animals and the environment once the detergents enter waterways. Find out what's in your detergent by checking the brand's website. If they don't list ingredients, ask them to send you the list. Check for toxins by googling 'Is ingredient X safe and non-toxic?' Choose a detergent with the fewest and safest ingredients, or consider making your own if you want to be sure it's non-toxic for you, your family and the environment.

Because detergents don't have 'toxic' written on the label, look for these keywords that are likely to be on the labels of safer detergents:[59]

- Biodegradable ingredients
- pH-neutral
- Cold water safe
- No phosphates
- Grey water suitable
- Plant-based surfactants
- Low sodium
- No microplastics
- No optical whiteners or brighteners
- Free from artificial fragrances and colours
- Allergy safe

Sheet, powder, liquid or pod

Buy sheet or powder detergent in recycled and recyclable cardboard packaging, rather than liquid in a plastic bottle. Liquid detergent contains a lot more water and their plastic containers aren't always recyclable or recycled. Detergent pods vary depending on the chemicals used to make them. Poisonings have occurred because they look a lot like confectionary, so they shouldn't be used in households with young children.

Use the right detergent for the fibre

Silk and wool prefer slightly acidic conditions, so silk-specific or gentle 'delicates' detergents are best to use. Gentle, non-toxic, eco dishwashing liquid is often pH-neutral, so I use this to handwash my silk and wool then add a dash of white cleaning vinegar to my rinse to return shine to silk and soften wool fibres. Cotton and linen can tolerate more alkaline conditions and rougher treatment. A standard, non-toxic laundry detergent will work for them.

Mild pH (meaning not too acidic or alkaline) detergent is better for you, your clothes and the environment. Harsh alkaline detergents can be abrasive on clothes, corroding them faster than mild detergents and increasing the chances of microplastic shedding and pollution.

Enzymes

Biological or non-biological refers to whether the detergent contains enzymes. Enzymes are added to detergent to digest fabric stains such as blood, oils, starches and fats. Their advantages are that they work in low temperatures, mild pH and small amounts. Their disadvantage is that they can cause allergic skin reactions in some people. Enzyme-based detergents are considered kinder to the environment than those containing phosphates because they are usually biodegradable. Check that enzyme-based detergents are suitable for sensitive skin before using them.

How much detergent is too much?

Only use the recommended amount of detergent or less. More detergent does not mean cleaner clothes! In fact, it can have the opposite effect and build up on clothes, attracting dirt and making clothes feel dirty when they're not.[60]

Washing machines

If you're shopping for a washing machine, look for the most energy-efficient one with the lowest water use. Make sure it does a short cycle and that you can control the temperature of cycles. And if it has a delicates cycle, great!

Use the lowest temperature you can; cold is best in terms of energy use and it's the gentlest on clothes. You can buy non-toxic detergent that works effectively in cold water. Washing in cold helps to avoid several issues.

A cold cycle is less likely to:

- shrink garments, especially wool
- make colours run
- release microplastics
- warp or damage garments
- cause fading.

Use the shortest cycle possible to get your clothes clean. Light, everyday soiling should be fine with a short wash. Some machines give you the option of soaking as part of the cycle, which is useful when you're dealing with very dirty clothes.

Dry-cleaning

Although dry-cleaning is a way to care for clothes that keeps them in circulation for longer, it also uses a lot of energy, and sometimes harmful chemicals. Dry-cleaning usually relies on chemical solvents to clean clothes, some of which are suspected to cause cancer and other issues.[61] The US Environmental Protection Agency states that dry-cleaning chemicals can cause air pollution when used without adequate air filtration. They have also been found to cause harm to dry-cleaning workers; however, relatively little research has been done on the risks of these chemicals to people who wear dry-cleaned clothes.[62]

There are alternatives to dry-cleaning using chemical solvents. One is a product called GreenEarth, which cleans with pure liquid silicone. Data is still lacking on the ongoing safety and environmental impacts of this product. Another is 'wet-cleaning', an industrial cleaning process that uses good-old water and detergent in specialised washing machines that carefully control water levels, agitation and temperature to ensure clothes aren't damaged. Although the process is gentler than washing in a domestic machine, wet-washing could still potentially damage clothes labelled 'dry-clean only'.

If you need to dry-clean, look for a 'green' dry-cleaner and ask if they:

- **use petrochemical-based solvents**
- **recycle their coat hangers**
- **wrap clothes in plastic (ask for no plastic)**
- **use low-energy machinery**
- **use renewable energy.**

You can also limit your use of dry-cleaning by spot-cleaning, airing out your clothes and using the wash-delay tactics in this chapter.[63]

Clothes dryers

Avoid clothes dryers if you can – they use a lot of energy and aren't kind to clothes. The best thing you can do for your clothes is to dry them outside in the fresh air if you have an outside washing line. Otherwise, drying inside on a clothing rack with a fan or dehumidifier will use less energy than a dryer and do less damage to your clothes.

Elastic is especially affected by heat and agitation, causing it to lose its stretch quickly. Using a dryer shortens the lifespan of our textiles and the dryer itself will end up in landfill at the end of its useful life. Sometimes using a dryer is unavoidable, but limiting its use as much as possible will reduce your energy use and prolong the life of your clothes.[64]

How to wash according to fibre type

Polyester and synthetics

If you already own synthetics, don't panic! You can wash them in a way that minimises their ongoing environmental impact. Keep these extra steps in mind before buying new synthetic clothing. You should be aware of its potential to cause harm to the environment (see pages 64–65) and be prepared to take responsibility for its proper care and recycling.

When washing synthetics such as polyester, elastane, acrylic and nylon, your main objective should be limiting the release of microfibres or microplastics into waterways. Remember, microplastics are small plastic fibres that shed during washing and cause harm to the environment. A single wash load can release several million microfibres.[65]

Reducing washing heat and agitation, and adding filtration, are the best ways to limit the release of microplastics. Here's how:

- Wash your synthetic clothing less – spot-clean it, spritz it or air it out instead.

- Machine-wash with a full load, which reduces agitation.

- Use a front-loading washing machine. These agitate clothing less forcefully than top-loaders.

- Handwash if possible, or use a short or delicates machine-wash cycle.

- Wash in cold water.

- Use the least possible amount of detergent and dissolve your powder detergent before use to reduce agitation.

- Use a lint filter.

- Get a microfilter washing bag, GuppyFriend bag or Cora Ball to capture microfibres in the wash. They're especially important to use when washing fleecy polyester items.

- Install an external microfibre filter on your washing machine or buy a machine with an inbuilt microfibre filter. Remember to clean the filter regularly and dispose of the contents with other solid waste, not down the drain.

- Dry synthetic clothing on the line rather than in the dryer.

Silk

You need to look after silk, but it's not as fragile as you might think. I recommend following the care instructions on your garment's label. If washing is okay, here's what to do. The main concern with silk is alkalinity, which can make silk brittle and dull. Most standard laundry soap is alkaline, so you need to use a pH-neutral detergent like eco dishwashing liquid, a delicates detergent or a silk-specific detergent.

- Follow care instructions on the label.

- If washing is okay, handwash or machine-wash your silk on the delicates cycle with a small amount of pH-neutral detergent.

- Use cold or lukewarm water.

- Soak silk overnight or squeeze it gently with your hands – don't rub it vigorously.

- Use 1 cup white cleaning vinegar in the rinse water to return silk to the slightly acidic conditions it loves. The vinegar helps the silk look soft and shiny.

- Treat stains in silk with vinegar or lemon juice – test on an inconspicuous area first to make sure colours aren't affected. For oil stains, use a gentle pH-neutral detergent on the stain, rubbing it gently then washing as usual.

- Dry your silk piece flat on a towel to make sure it keeps its shape.

- Iron on low temperature. Silk doesn't like getting too hot. If you have a steamer, this can be used to get creases out without damaging the fabric.

Wool

Have you ever accidentally shrunk your favourite woollen jumper or beanie? It's heart-breaking, but so easy to avoid. Heat, soap and agitation are the perfect conditions to create felt, which is *not* what we want when we're washing our favourite jumper! So keep heat low, use gentle soap and wash with as little agitation as possible.

- Follow care instructions on the label.

- Wool doesn't like temperature shock, so be careful not to use water that's too hot; lukewarm is best. The water should be the same temperature as your skin.

- Use a gentle pH-neutral eco dishwashing liquid, eco-friendly woolwash or delicates detergent.

- Don't be rough when washing, just gently squeeze the water through the fibres. Leaving the garment to soak for a few hours or overnight will help get your wool lovely and clean without being rough.

- Handwashing is safest with wool, but if you have a delicates or wool cycle on your machine, you could use it if your garment's care label specifies that gentle machine-washing is okay, although I'd recommend testing it on something other than your favourite jumper the first time you use it.

- Rinse in lukewarm water until the water is clear. Adding a cup of white cleaning vinegar at this point will keep your wool soft and give it a beautiful shine. Rinse out the vinegar.

- Gently squeeze out the excess water.

- Lay your wool garment flat on a towel to dry – this will stop it stretching out of shape.

- Never iron your wool with a hot iron; use a low temperature setting.

Cotton

Cotton is breathable and easy to care for, making it one of the world's most popular fibres. It's a hardy fibre that can handle heat and fairly rough treatment. Here's how to wash it to keep it looking fab.

- Follow care instructions on the label.

- Spot-clean between washes.

- Use the short or 'eco' cycle on your machine.

- Only wash full loads to minimise agitation.

- Wash with similar colours.

- Wash cotton in cold water – it's better for the environment and your clothes will be just as clean!

- Use eco-friendly, low-phosphorus washing detergents and only use as much as the instructions suggest.

- Hang your cottons on the line to dry – this will save you energy, reduce the risk of shrinkage and keep them looking good for longer.

Denim

Most denim is made from a high percentage of cotton, which is sometimes blended with elastic fibre for stretch jeans. Denim is particularly susceptible to fading and shrinkage, so follow the cotton instructions for jeans but add these steps to preserve the shape and colour of your indigo blues for as long as possible.

- Follow care instructions on the label.

- Spot-clean or air out between washes. Denim doesn't need washing after every wear.

- Cold wash denim inside out.

- Dry on the line inside out.

- Use minimal detergent.

- Don't tumble dry.

- Handwash to prevent fading.

- For longevity, choose pure cotton jeans.[66]

Linen

Humans have used this hardy fabric for thousands of years, long before washing machines. These tricks will help you keep it looking good over time.

- Follow care instructions on the label.

- Use lukewarm water to handwash or machine-wash on a delicates cycle.

- Use a mild detergent – woolwash works!

- Don't bleach your linen or it will become brittle.

- Don't overload the washing machine – this will cause tangles and wrinkles, and be tough on the fabric.

- The heat and agitation of using a dryer will shorten the life of your linen. If you need to use a dryer, use a low heat setting.

- Dry your linen on the line and spread it out flat to reduce wrinkles.

- Ironing linen while it's still slightly damp makes it easier to get creases out.

Rayon

Rayon fabrics such as modal, Tencel, lyocell, cupro, acetate, viscose and bamboo rayon aren't resilient to heat and can get brittle unless washed with care. These fabrics are also prone to warping and damage in the washing machine so handwashing is best.

- Follow care instructions on the label.

- A gentle handwash is better than machine-washing for rayon.

- Use a small amount of gentle detergent; don't use bleach or fabric softeners.

- Wash in cold or lukewarm water.

- Never put rayon in the dryer; dry it on the line or lay it flat on a towel.

- Don't twist or wring it out.

CHAPTER 11: CLOTHING MAINTENANCE

Clothing maintenance is easy when you chip away at it regularly. I collect everything that needs love into a basket, which I pull out when I'm having a lazy night in front of a movie. I love giving my hands something to do while I'm sitting still, and there's nothing like the satisfaction of working through a pile of jobs while watching something trashy. It feels like cheating somehow.

Removing pills

If your knitwear is covered in pills or bobbles – those fuzzy balls that develop on the surface of woolly clothing – don't throw it away. A bit of maintenance can be therapeutic for you and your clothing!

You can pick the pills off by hand if you have the time and inclination. I don't recommend using a razor because it's too easy to accidentally slice through your favourite jumper.

Lots of gadgets are out there to make the de-pilling process easier. I prefer using an electric fabric shaver. These have little blades inside a protective case with holes in it just big enough for the pills to stick through and be neatly sliced off. To avoid making holes, make sure you lay your garment flat. Methodically work your way over one side of your garment, then flip it over and do the other side. Focus on the underarm areas and sleeves because these areas are most likely to get pills due to friction.

Take your time and enjoy the methodical process. Feel good about yourself for maintaining your clothes and saving them from landfill.

Brushing

A good way to remove dust and lint from your clothing is by brushing it. You can buy clothes brushes from fabric stores or online clothing-care companies. Using a brush is safer than using a sticky-roll lint remover because it won't leave adhesive residue on your clothes and creates a lot less waste. Brushing is great for winter jackets and clothing that gets stored for long periods between uses. For fuzzy items, it's a gentle way of combing fibres to ensure they stay glossy and looking as good as new.

Moths and pests

Staying on top of pests in your wardrobe can save your clothes from disastrous infestations. Clothes moths can move in without you even noticing, and by the time you pull out your favourites for the cold season, they can be full of holes. While these holes are fixable, here are some ways to stop them from happening in the first place.

Make sure your clothes are put away clean. If you're packing things away for a season, wash, spritz or air items first so they don't attract insects. Make sure they are put away dry and stored in a dry place.

Don't use harsh chemicals to prevent or treat insect infestations – these might end up being toxic for you and your family. Plenty of natural moth and insect repellents are available to keep your clothes safe. Check your local health-food store for moth traps or natural repellents, or read on for a way to make your own.

MOTH REPELLENT BAG PROJECT

||||||||||||||||||||||||||||||||||||||||||||||||||||||||||||||||||||||||||||||||||||||||||||||||

This easy project is a great one for kids to have a go at when they're learning to sew.

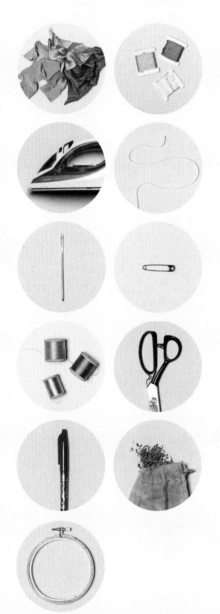

Difficulty rating:
Easy

Time needed:
1 hour

What to upcycle: Old sheets, pillowslips or lightweight cotton summer clothes would make great fabric scraps to use for this project

What you'll need

18 x 25 cm (7 x 10 inch) natural fibre fabric scrap (loose weave is better so the moth-repelling smells can escape the bag)

Iron

Sewing needle

Thread

Moth template to trace

Erasable fabric pen

Embroidery hoop

4–5 colours of embroidery threads, 1 metre (3¼ feet) each

60 cm (24 inch) piece of string

Safety pin

Scissors

Dried lavender flowers to fill the bag

MOTH TEMPLATE

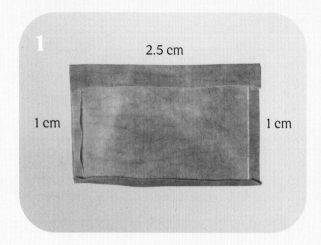

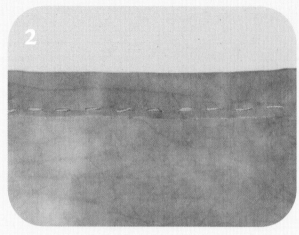

1. Fold 1 cm (⅓ inch) of each short side back and iron them flat. Fold over 2.5 cm (1 inch) of the top edge and iron it flat. Fold over 1 cm (⅓ inch) of the bottom edge and iron it flat.

2. Stitch the top folded edge with a running stitch 2 cm (¾ inch) from the edge of the fabric.

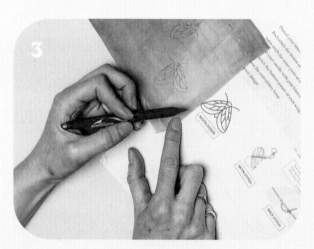

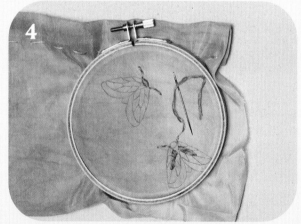

3. Using an erasable fabric marker, trace the moth template provided on the previous page.

4. Embroider your moth with one colour per panel, using a satin stitch. You can trace and embroider as many moths as you can fit on a bag! For detailed instructions on how to embroider the moth, see pages 132–133.

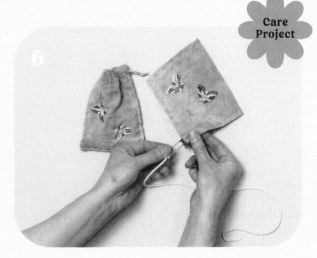

5. Fold your piece of fabric in half with right sides facing out. Pin the sides together leaving the top 2 cm (1 inch) free. Stitch down the right side of the fabric and across the bottom using a running stitch.

6. Tie your string onto the safety pin and thread it through the channel at the top of the fabric. Once it's out the other side, make sure it's even on both sides and tie the two ends of string together in a knot.

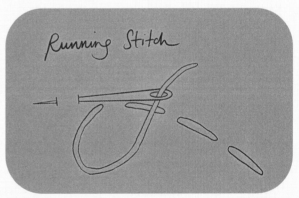

Running Stitch

7. Fill your drawstring bag with any of the following moth-repelling items: camphor laurel wood scraps, cedar wood scraps, lavender, bay leaves, cloves, rosemary, thyme, cotton wool balls or fabric scraps with drops of eucalyptus or cedar essential oil. Replace the contents of the moth bag every six months to keep the smells strong.

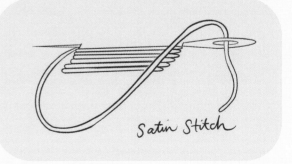

Satin Stitch

Clothing maintenance 99

Damp

Mould and mildew can discolour clothes, and natural fibres will start to biodegrade if they're kept warm and damp. Insects also love these conditions, so it's important to keep your clothing dry.

If you live in a humid place, put damp absorbers into your wardrobe to absorb moisture. Even if you don't live somewhere humid, airing out your wardrobe regularly is a great idea. If it's a sunny day and you have time to hang your clothes out in the sun for a few hours every season, this will help to keep damp, insects and bacteria levels down.

Bicarbonate of soda (baking soda) is a great damp absorber that will also get rid of musty smells. Put it at the bottom of your wardrobe in a bowl or container with holes in it. Don't forget to replace it after a few months or when it gets hard. You can add a few drops of insect-repelling essential oils, such as lavender, clove, rosemary, thyme, eucalyptus or cedar, to keep your clothes smelling great.

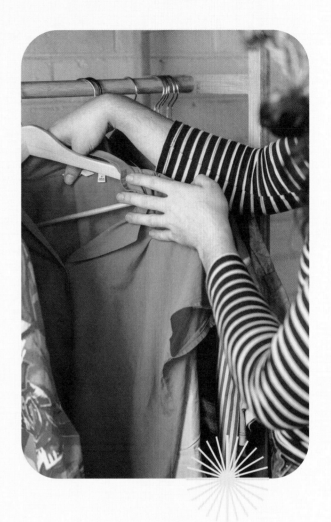

Caring for your clothes has a HUGE impact on how long they last, and it's worth the effort. There's no better way to honour the skills, resources and energy required to create these wonderful pieces than lovingly caring for them so that they can live on.

SECTION 3

KEEP

This section aims to inspire you to keep your clothes. We know that making new clothes uses more resources than the planet can sustain. We also know that fashion manufacturing and waste are some of the world's biggest polluters. The clothing you already own is valuable treasure that you've collected for a reason. Seeing the value embedded in it means acknowledging and respecting the resources and labour it took to make these garments.

Keeping your clothes in circulation is an active way to show you care for the planet that provided the materials for them and the people who made them. It's a way of refusing to contribute to the massive textile waste problem that mostly affects those who can least afford it. It's an act of resistance to fashion marketing, which is constantly telling you to buy more clothes. So, instead of heading to the shops for new clothes, shop your own wardrobe first. Chances are, it's full of untapped potential and much-loved pieces you can bring back into circulation.

CHAPTER 12: LOVE YOUR WARDROBE BACK TO LIFE

'A garment mended multiple times reads like a photo album, with the moments and memories that we stitch upon our clothes' —Orsola de Castro, in Loved Clothes Last

We've already looked at how much we have in our wardrobes (see Chapter 1: Do you need it?, pages 18–23) and some of us, including me, have discovered that we have a lot more than we realised. The next project, 'Wardrobe revolution', guides you through the process of organising the items in your wardrobe into categories that inspire action, so you can make the most of what you have. Instead of discarding what you're not wearing or what's broken, this project is the first step towards transforming it into something you'll love. If you really need to pass things on, I'll show you how to do this thoughtfully and responsibly.

It's a good idea to do this project on the same day as the wardrobe stocktake project in Chapter 1 (see pages 22–23), to minimise the number of times you'll need to pull out all your clothes. It's fun to do this with a friend, with music playing and snacks to keep you going. Give yourself plenty of time. Set aside at least half a day to do this project so you don't feel rushed. You could offer to do the same for your friend as a swap.

Project: Wardrobe revolution

1. Clear a spot on the floor or your bed for four piles with a sticky note marking each pile:

   - Perfect as they are
   - Fix
   - Change
   - Pass it on

2. Go through your hanging items first and select your 'Perfect as they are' items. Pull them out and put them on the first pile. (For ideas on what to do with this pile, see Chapter 13: The 'Perfect as they are' pile, page 109.)

3. Next, pull out anything needing repairs and put it in the 'Fix' pile. (See Chapter 14: The 'Fix' pile, pages 110–148.)

4. Pull out the pieces that you love but don't work in their current form – maybe you love the fabric but there's an issue with the fit. Put these into the 'Change' pile. (See Chapter 15: The 'Change' pile, pages 150–198.)

5. Whatever's left should be items for the 'Pass it on' pile. (See Chapter 16: The 'Pass it on' pile, pages 200–207.)

A note on keeping 'aspirational' clothing

Do you have an item in your wardrobe that you're keeping for the day your body will be the right shape for it? Does it make you feel bad about yourself every time you look at it? I encourage you to pass on these items. My philosophy is that our clothes should fit the bodies we have right now and should definitely *not* make us feel guilty, bad or wrong. Our clothes should do the opposite!

Things to consider while you're sorting through your clothes:

- What did I love about this when I collected it?

- What was my reason for buying it initially?

- What memories are attached to it – the day I got it or times I've worn it? What does it make me think of?

- What do I like about wearing it? How does it make me feel?

- Does it fit?

- Does it need fixing?

- Could it be turned into something else?

- Would it work in a different colour?

- How often do I wear it? How long since it was last worn?

- What stops me from wearing it?

- Does it work with three other items?

CHAPTER 13: THE 'PERFECT AS THEY ARE' PILE

Items that are already in high rotation, make you feel great and get used a couple of times a week are considered perfect as they are. You can return these items to your wardrobe. But before you do, have a think about what makes them perfect. There will be recurring traits running through the items you love. What are they? Consider what puts them in this category, write down exactly what works about them and refer to that list whenever you're considering replacing something.

Usually, these items fit us well, feel good on our bodies, are a colour that suit us and get us compliments when we're wearing them. These are clothes we feel confident in. They might not be the latest style – they might even be decades old – but this feeling is how all of our clothes should make us feel. These pieces need to become your classic style, regardless of fashion trends and marketing pressure. This is your 'uniform'. (For more on how to find your classic style, see the style play project on pages 28–33.)

It might be worth having a local dressmaker take a pattern from special pieces so you can get more made as the old ones wear out. Is this what will inspire you to learn how to sew so you can make one in every colour?

The clothes I come back to time and again often have the following traits:

- Made from natural fibres
- Utilitarian style
- Vintage or a good example of handiwork
- Simple
- High-waisted
- Wide leg
- Button-down or V-neck
- Colours – pale pink, denim blues, dusty greens, black, white and dark red

When I need to look for something, I look for things that fit this profile. This is my 'perfect' list. Once you've written your list, return these items to your wardrobe and move on to the next pile.

CHAPTER 14: THE 'FIX' PILE

Put items into the 'Fix' pile that are in good condition apart from having something that stops you wearing them. Maybe it's a missing button, fallen-down hem, split seam, broken zip or small hole. Maybe it's a pair of shoes that need resoling. Whatever the issue is, you've probably been meaning to get it fixed for ages. Now is the time to do it!

For something you're not confident fixing yourself, take it to your local alterations shop. This is often cheaper than replacing the item, you'll be supporting a local business and you'll keep the item out of landfill – triple win!

If you want to have a go at fixing the issue yourself, read on for instructions. For anything not listed in this chapter, search online for the issue plus 'repair' and you're sure to find an instructional video on how to do it.

Basic repair kit

Everyone should have some basic repair items at home. You can find these tools at most supermarkets and all sewing shops. They're usually inexpensive and if you'd like to become a regular mender, they'll be endlessly useful:

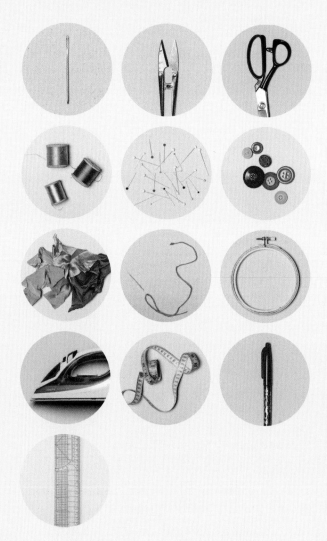

- Sewing needles
- Thread snips
- Scissors
- Threads in different colours
- Pins
- Buttons
- Fabric scraps
- Wool yarn scraps
- Embroidery hoop
- Iron and ironing board
- Tape measure
- Heat-erasable markers
- Ruler

If you want to get more involved with repairs and sewing projects, these items will make great additions to your kit:

- Sewing machine
- Darning mushroom
- Quick unpick tool

'Fix' projects

The following projects address some of the common reasons people give me for why they throw items of clothing into the bin.

It may take a little time to work through your 'Fix' pile, but keep your eyes on the prize. Once you've finished, you'll have a bunch of fully functioning, wearable clothes to put back into your wardrobe. Mix and match these items with your 'Perfect as they are' clothes.

Investing your time, energy and creativity into the repair process creates a beautiful feedback loop that makes clothes feel even more valuable than before. You may have just turned something into a family heirloom, and by learning these skills, you've saved an item from landfill. You should be feeling like a hero.

SEW ON A BUTTON

||||||||||||||||||||||||||||||||||||||||||||||||||||

Difficulty rating:
Easy

Time needed:
20 minutes

What you'll need

Needle

Thread

Thread snips

Buttons

Erasable fabric marker

1. Cut 1 metre (3¼ feet) sewing thread in a colour similar to the thread used on the other buttons. Thread your needle, doubling the thread, and tie a knot in the end.

2. If you can't see where the button has come off, use the marker to make a small mark on the fabric where the button needs to go. Bring your needle up through the fabric from the left of the mark to the right.

3. Place the button onto the fabric, centred over your mark, and bring the needle through the hole in the button from the back to the front. Cross over to the hole horizontally opposite and push your needle through the hole in the button then the fabric, from front to back. Bring your needle through your mark from back to front again, repeating this sequence at least three times. If your button has four holes, repeat the same process for the bottom row of holes.

4. Once you feel your button is solidly attached, bring your needle through the button to the back of the fabric. Sew three tiny stitches in the same place to secure your thread, then snip your thread.

SEW UP A HEM (HAND-STITCHED HERRINGBONE HEM)

‖‖‖

Take note of how the hem was sewn originally and try to make your stitches as similar as possible. If your hem is machine-stitched, you can still hand-sew hem repairs. Otherwise, you may want to machine-stitch the hem yourself or take it to an alterations shop if you feel you want the hem repair to match the original hem exactly. These instructions are for a good all-round hemming technique called herringbone stitch, which is almost invisible from the front and works well on lots of different garments.

Difficulty rating:
Medium

Time needed:
1 hour

What you'll need

Iron

Tape measure

Pins

Needle

Thread

Thread snips

1. Iron your hems to where they need to be, so they are flat and sitting in the right place. You can also pin your hem to keep it in place for sewing. Cut 1 metre (3¼ feet) sewing thread in a similar colour to the piece of clothing you're repairing. Thread your needle, doubling the thread, and tie a knot in the end.

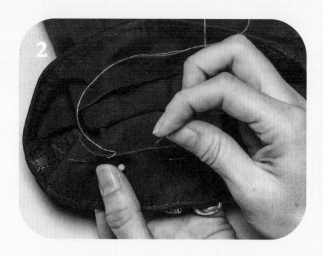 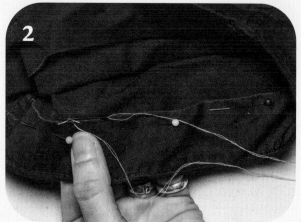

2. Bring your needle up from inside the hem and diagonally up to the right by 1 cm (⅓ inch). With the point of your needle pointing to the left, take a small stitch from the top of the hem.

 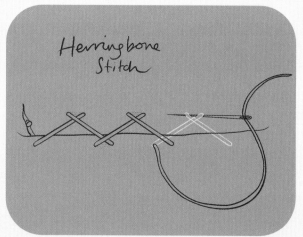

3. Check whether your stitching is visible from the front. If it is, take out that stitch and try again until you're taking such a small stitch that you can't see it from the front.

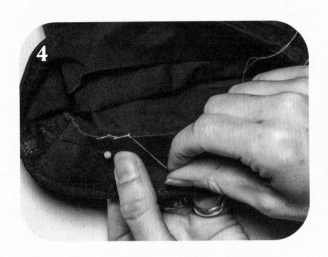

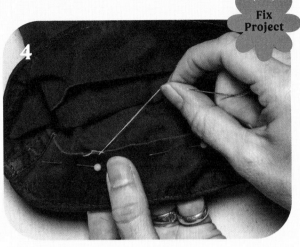

4. Cross diagonally downwards over your original stitch by 1 cm (⅓ inch) and, with your needle pointing to the left, take a small stitch from the bottom of the hem.

Cross diagonally upwards and to the right over your last stitch by 1 cm (⅓ inch). With your needle pointing to the left, take a small stitch from the top of the hem.

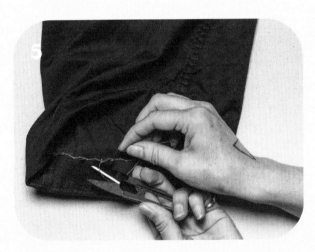

5. Repeat this process until you have sewn the whole way around the hem. Make sure you keep checking whether you can see any of your stitches from the front. If you're happy with how it looks, make three small stitches to secure the end of your thread and snip.

The 'Fix' pile   119

REPAIR A SPLIT SEAM
||||||||||||||||||||||||||||||||||||||||||||||||||||||||||

How you repair a split seam varies depending on what the garment is made of and how it was stitched. A good general rule with repairs is to let the garment be your guide – copy the way it was made originally. If possible, use the same kind of stitches and thread. If this isn't possible, or hard to work out, this stitch will close up a split seam by hand.

Difficulty rating:
Easy

Time needed:
30 minutes

What you'll need

Needle

Thread

Thread snips

Pins

1. Cut 1 metre (3¼ feet) sewing thread in a similar colour to the piece of clothing you're repairing. Thread your needle with a double thread and tie both ends together with a knot.

2. Turn your garment inside out and lay it flat so the split seam is facing you. Place both sides of the split seam together and pin in place. Make sure you're pinning along the same line that it was previously stitched and that the front and back seam lines match up.

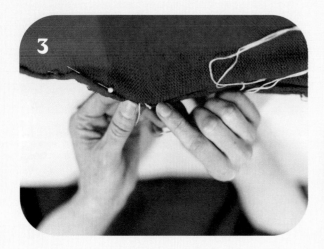

3. Start your repair at least 5 cm (2 inches) away from the split (within the section that hasn't split). Bring your needle from the back of the fabric to the front along the seam line.

4. Moving from right to left (if you're right-handed), make a 5 mm (¼ inch) stitch by pushing your needle through both layers of fabric from the front and bringing it out at the back. From the back, bring your needle to the front of the fabric, leaving a 1 cm (⅓ inch) gap from where you came out at the back. This is called a backstitch.

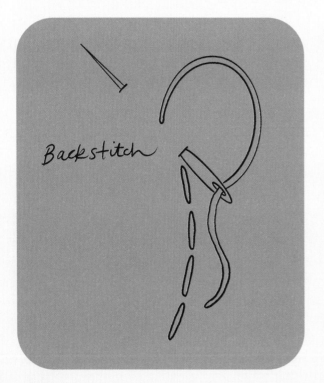

Backstitch

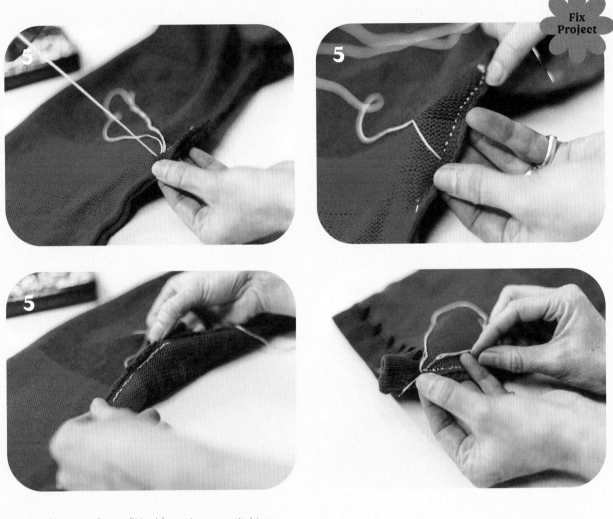

5. You'll have a 5 mm (¼ inch) gap in your stitching
line from the front, so take your needle to the right
and push it back through the end of your first stitch
from front to back. Repeat this until you are 5 cm
(2 inches) past the split. Once you've finished,
secure your thread with three tiny stitches in
the same place and snip your thread.

DARN A HOLE

Darning is a fantastic way to reinforce and repair knitted garments. It's perfect for socks and jumpers, and looks fantastic as a feature mend in a bright or contrasting yarn colour. In a matching colour, a darn can look almost invisible.

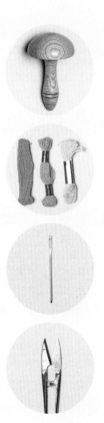

Difficulty rating:
Medium

Time needed:
Depends on the size of the hole, from 1 hour for a small hole to many hours for a large one.

What you'll need

Darning mushroom (if you don't have one, try using a jar or ball)

Yarn of a similar weight to the yarn that has been used to knit the garment

Needle

Thread snips

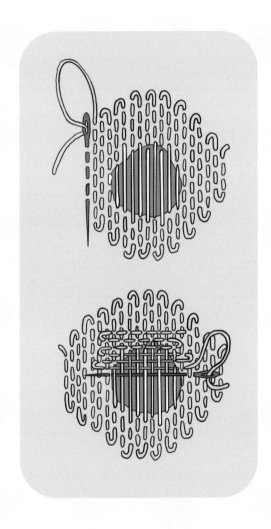

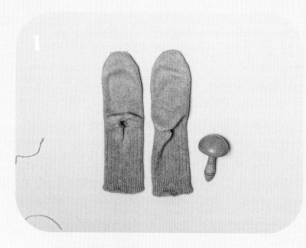

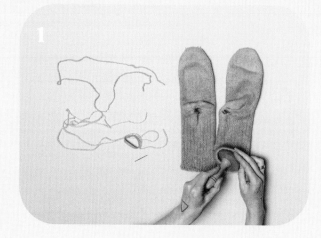

1. Turn your sock or jumper inside out and work on the inside of the hole. Position the hole over the darning mushroom. Make sure your fabric isn't stretched.

2. Tidy the edges of the hole by snipping away long threads and messy edges if needed.

3. Cut 1 metre (3¼ feet) yarn or thread (of a similar weight to what you're mending). Thread your needle with a single thread, tie a knot in one end and leave a tail at the other.

4. Start your darn 2–3 cm (approx. 1 inch) away from the edge of the hole into the body of the garment. This will strengthen the entire area.

5. First, stitch vertical lines with a running stitch, leaving a gap as wide as the thread you are using for the repair in between your rows. Keep a small amount of thread as a loop at the end of each row so that your darn is able to stretch a little.

6. Once you finish the first row, turn around and make a second row, close to the first. Don't pull your threads too tightly.

7. Alternate your stitches with the spaces from the row before. Pick up the edge of the hole in one row, then go over the edge of the row in the next one.

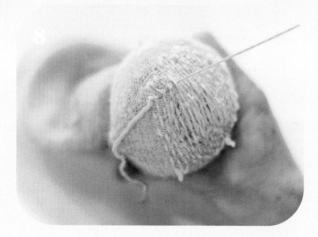

8.   Once you've gone 2–3 cm (approx. 1 inch) past the edge of the hole, secure your thread with three small stitches in the same place, then snip your thread.

9.   Tie another knot in your thread and start stitching your horizontal darning lines, 1 cm (⅓ inch) away from the edge of the hole. Weave your needle over and under each vertical darning thread as you go. Alternate under and over each darning thread on your next row. With this action you are actually weaving new fabric to fill the hole in your garment!

10.   Once you've completed your darn 1 cm (⅓ inch) past the edge of the hole, secure your thread with three small stitches in the same place and snip your thread.

MOTH MEND FOR A MOTH HOLE

Here's a fun way to turn holes on your jumpers into beautiful decorations. This is my friend Amber's favourite jumper, which had been chewed on by moths. I decided to cover the biggest hole with a moth embroidery as a cheeky nod to the species we sometimes share our clothes with.

Difficulty rating:
Medium to advanced

Time needed:
3–4 hours

What you'll need

An adhesive, water-soluble stabiliser

Erasable fabric marker

Moth template to trace

Needle

Scissors

Embroidery threads in yellow, pink, green and blue

Bucket

Water

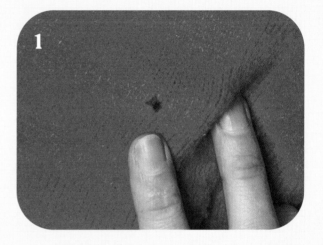

1. If the hole in your garment is bigger than 2 cm (¾ inch) diameter, reinforce the hole first with a darn, following the instructions on pages 125–128.

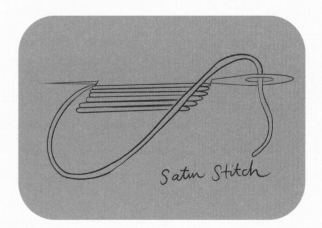

Satin Stitch

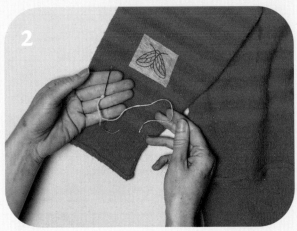

2. Trace or print your moth using the template on page 97 onto an adhesive, water-soluble stabiliser. This is available in sewing shops or online. Stick the stabiliser onto your fabric, making sure the entire hole is covered. Alternatively, draw the moth directly onto the garment using an erasable fabric marker.

Thread your needle with yellow thread (use all six strands of thread), leaving a tail, and tie a knot in the end.

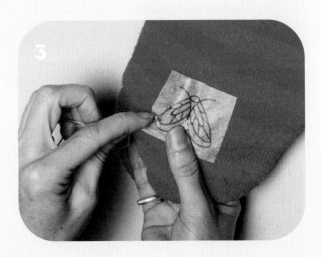

3. Satin-stitch the head, the top of the moth's body, the sides of each wing and the base of the body as shown.

When you finish all the yellow sections, sew three tiny stitches in the same place on the inside of the garment and snip your threads. Repeat this as you finish each colour.

132 Keep

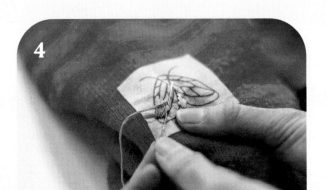

4. Thread your needle with pink thread and tie a knot in the end. Satin-stitch the sides and centre of each wing.

5. Thread your needle with green thread. Satin-stitch the inner of each wing.

6. Thread your needle with blue thread. Backstitch the feelers of the moth and satin-stitch the last panels of each wing.

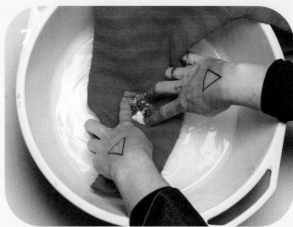

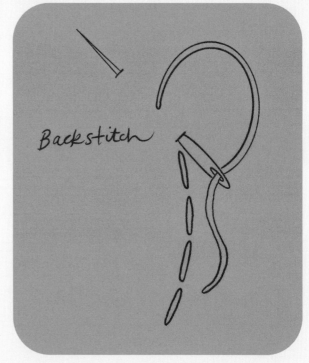

Backstitch

7. To dissolve your template, fill a bucket with a small amount of water. Submerge your moth, gently rubbing the stabiliser away until it no longer feels sticky. Gently squeeze out the excess water and lay your garment flat to dry.

PATCH A HOLE

IIIIIIIIIIIIIIIIIIIIIIIIIIIIIIIIIIIIII

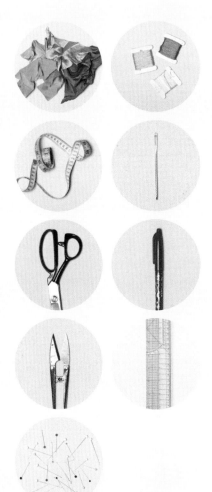

Difficulty rating:
Medium

Time needed:
3–4 hours

What to upcycle: For patch fabrics, use a similar weight of fabric to the item you're patching: old denim jeans or heavy cotton chinos for denim repairs, or stretch fabrics like old T-shirts to repair stretch clothing

What you'll need

Patch fabric

Tape measure

Scissors

Thread snips

Pins

Embroidery threads

Needle

Erasable marker

Ruler

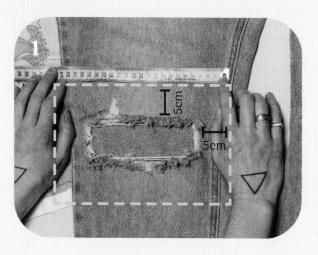

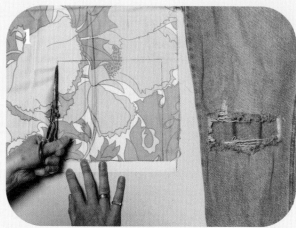

1. Measure the hole to make sure your patch is big enough to cover the hole you are mending and at least 5 cm (2 inches) bigger than the hole on all sides. Once you know the size, cut out your patch.

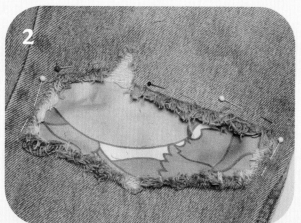

2. Neaten the edges of the hole by trimming any long threads. This makes a tidy edge, which is much easier to sew! Place your patch fabric inside the leg of the jeans and pin it in place.

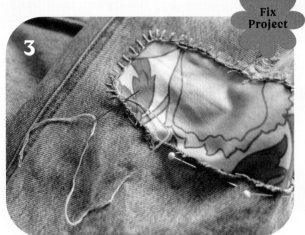

3. Thread your needle, leaving a tail and tying a knot in the end. Use all six strands of embroidery thread. Blanket stitch around the edge of the hole.

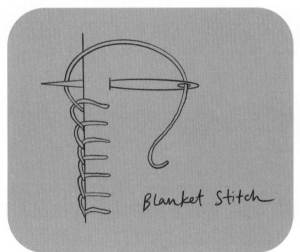

Blanket Stitch

4. Once the patch has been stitched all the way around, add more decorative running stitches to reinforce the edges of your patch. Mark these with an erasable marker or chalk. It can help to use a ruler to draw them in.

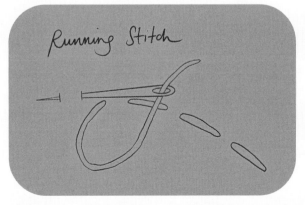

Running Stitch

The 'Fix' pile 139

REPLACE A WORN-OUT SHIRT COLLAR

Worn-out shirt collars are common, and it's no wonder when you think about the wear and tear they're exposed to every day. Sweat, sunscreen, sun and friction on our collars mean they're often the first place to wear out. Before you throw that shirt in the bin, however, give this project a go. You'll not only repair your shirt, but also add a personal touch.

You'll need to use fabric of a similar weight to what was originally used to make the shirt. If you're feeling adventurous, you might decide to introduce bright colours or patterns to a boring shirt. Check whether you have something usable in your collected fabric scraps before buying new fabric for this project.

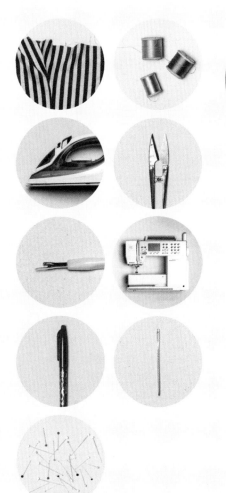

Difficulty rating:
Advanced

Time needed:
5 hours

What to upcycle: Old shirt fabric, sheets or pillowslips – any fabric of a similar weight to the collar you're replacing

What you'll need

Fabric scraps

Iron

Quick unpick tool

Heat-erasable marker

Iron-on interfacing (optional)

Pins

Thread

Thread snips

Sewing machine

Sewing needle

NOTE: You can stitch this project on a sewing machine if you have one, or hand-stitch if you don't. Use a backstitch (see page 122) to join the collar pieces and a running stitch (see page 139) for top-stitching.

1. Find a piece of fabric that's at least twice as big as your shirt collar and stand, plus 1 cm (⅓ inch) extra all the way around for seam allowance. Iron it flat and put it aside.

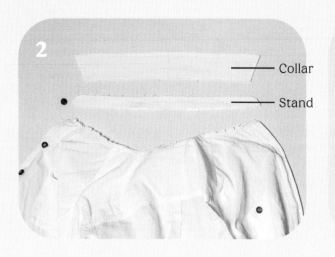

Collar

Stand

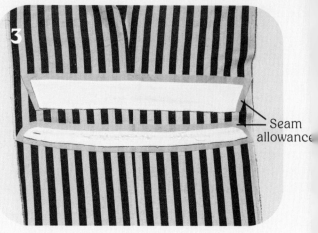

Seam
allowance

2. Unpick your collar from the neck of the shirt, and the collar from the stand, being careful not to damage the fabric of the shirt.

3. Use your unpicked collar pieces as patterns by laying them flat on your fabric scrap. Add 1 cm (⅓ inch) seam allowance all sides except the base of the collar.

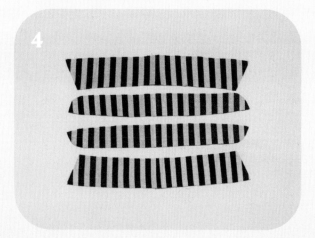

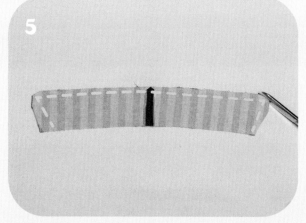

4. Cut out two of each collar piece and two of each stand piece.

5. Lay both collar pieces with right sides together and stitch around the left side, top and right side, 1 cm (⅓ inch) from the edge of the fabric. Leave the bottom edge unstitched. Once you've stitched it, snip the edges of the collar 3 mm (⅛ inch) from the edge of your sewing line. This makes the collar points nice and pointy when you turn them right side out.

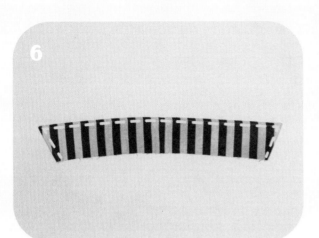

6. Turn your collar right side out and iron it flat. Make sure the points of the collar are properly turned through – use a pencil tip to get right into the corner. If the original collar has a line of stitching about 5 mm (¼ inch) from the edge, you can add that too through all layers.

7. Iron under the seam allowances of your collar stand. Mark the centre of the collar with your erasable marker. Do the same with the collar-stand pieces, then sandwich the collar between the collar-stand pieces, matching centre marks and pinning in place. Stitch the collar to the stand and iron everything flat.

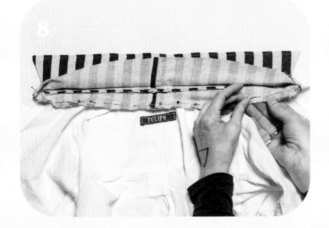

8. Pin the back layer of the collar stand onto the neckline of the shirt, then stitch this line.

9. Pin the final edge of the stand. Stitch this down and, hooray, you have a new collar and your shirt is wearable for many more years to come!

REPLACE ELASTIC

|||||||||||||||||||||||||||||||||||||||||||||||||

If your elastic has lost its spring, here's how to replace it to keep your waistline in the right place and your clothes usable.

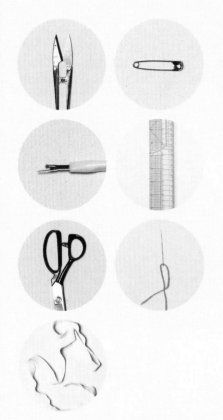

Difficulty rating:
Easy

Time needed:
30 minutes

NOTE: Check whether your local fabric recyclers accept worn-out elastic; most don't. If not, keep it for garden ties or rope. Most elastic is synthetic and derived from plastic, so it shouldn't be thrown in the bin.

What you'll need

Thread snips

Quick unpick tool

Scissors

Biodegradable elastic, enough to fit around your waist plus 5 cm (2 inch) seam allowance

Large safety pin

Ruler

Needle and thread

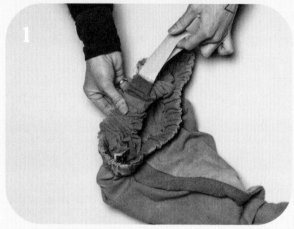

1. With your quick unpick tool, open a small split on the inside of your waistband to access the old elastic. Pull out a loop of elastic, cut through it and pull it completely out of the channel.

2. Give your new piece of elastic a good stretch. Make sure you have enough to fit comfortably around your waist – don't forget to allow about 5 cm (2 inches) extra for seam allowance so the elastic can overlap and be stitched together.

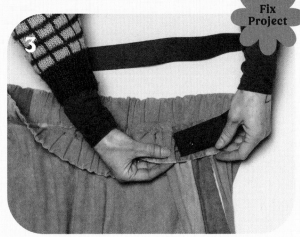

3. Put the safety pin through one end of the new elastic. Poke the loaded safety pin through the split in the waistband and feed the elastic all the way around the channel and out the split again. Make sure the elastic is sitting flat the whole way through the channel, not twisted.

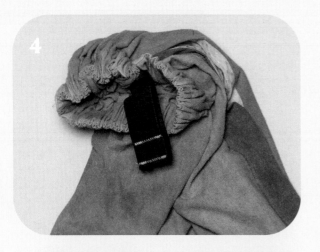

Whip Stitch

4. Pin the edges of the elastic together, overlapping
the edges by 2.5 cm (1 inch), again making sure you
haven't twisted the elastic. Hand- or machine-stitch
the elastic together using strong thread and lots of
stitches. Once it's sewn together, pull the waist tight
so the elastic pops back into the channel. Check
again that the elastic isn't twisted. Hand-stitch the
split in the waistband closed using a whip stitch.

CHAPTER 15: THE 'CHANGE' PILE

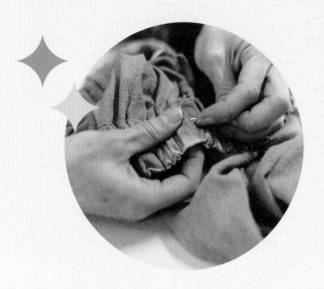

The following projects will help you work through your 'Change' pile. Don't let the current form of your clothing restrict you. If you love the fabric but want a new shape, or if it's too worn-out in places to stay as it is, let your imagination run wild and turn it into something else! Once you're done, you'll have a bunch of clothes to return to your wardrobe, or some useful items for the home, ready to be used for many more years to come.

The 'Change' pile is for items that don't work in their current form. This includes garments that:

- need to be let out or taken in so they fit you

- have stains that won't budge so need to be dyed a new colour

- need to be transformed. (You love the fabric they're made from but would wear it more in a different shape.)

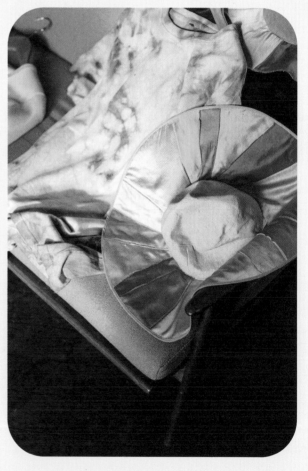

OVER-DYE A STAIN

||||||||||||||||||||||||||||||||||||||||||||||||

If you've got an item of clothing or a pillowslip with a stain that won't budge, this project is for you. Don't throw the item away, refresh it with a new natural colour every season! This project shows you how to make just one of the endless colours we can get from nature. Once you've tried this colour, experiment with others for a non-toxic colour revolution.

This dye will work on any natural fibre fabric, like cotton T-shirts or cotton or linen pillowslips. Before starting, make sure the fabric you're dyeing has been well washed. New fabric will need a couple of washes before it can absorb dye. This recipe will make enough dye for two to three T-shirts or pillowslips.

Difficulty rating:
Easy

Time needed:
2 days

What to upcycle: Stained shirts or T-shirts, pillowslips, bedsheets

What you'll need

10-litre (2½ gallon) aluminium or stainless-steel pot

A large bouquet of fresh eucalyptus or oak leaves (enough to fill your pot)

5–10 rusted nails or other rusted metal items

Spoon

Tongs

Ball of cotton string

Scissors

Natural fibre item to dye

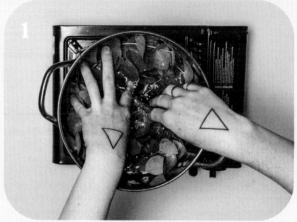

1. Add the fresh eucalyptus or oak leaves to your pot and cover them with water. Try to fit as many leaves as you can into the pot. Bring the pot to a simmer on your stove then keep it simmering for 3 hours, stirring occasionally. Remove from the heat. Let the solution cool down overnight. This will be your dyebath.

2. While your pot is simmering, lay your dry T-shirt flat on a table and scrunch it evenly into a round but flat pancake shape, keeping the front of the T-shirt facing up. Keep scrunching until your fabric piece is compact enough to fit into your saucepan. Tie your string in a loop around the fabric, making sure you keep the pancake as flat as possible. Leave out a tail of string for tying the other end later. Keep wrapping the string around the fabric until you have a compact, flat, circular bundle that stays together when you lift it up. Tie the end of the string to the tail you've left out.

NOTE: Soaking your fabric in soy milk overnight before dyeing will make natural dye colours bright and long-lasting. Squeeze out excess milk after soaking, hang it to dry on the line and it's ready to dye!

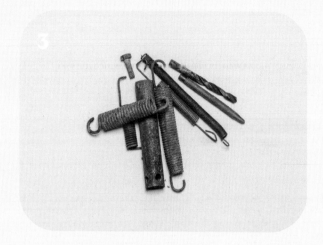

3. Add your rusty items to a bucket filled with just enough cold water to cover the rusty items, then add your bundled T-shirt and leave it to soak overnight.

4. In the morning, check the colour of the dyebath – it should look like a nice brew of Ceylon tea. If not, repeat the simmering process. Once you get a nice strong colour from your leaves, fish them out of the pot with tongs and put them in the compost bin. Your dyebath is ready!

5. Remove your T-shirt bundle from the rusty water and place it into the dyebath, making sure it is covered with dye. Bring your dyebath to a simmer and keep it simmering for 3 hours, turning the T-shirt over occasionally. Turn off the heat and leave the bundle to sit in the dyebath overnight.

6. In the morning, take your bundle out of the dyebath and squeeze out the excess dye. Snip your threads to unravel your bundle and reveal the amazing design you've created!

7. Handwash your fabric gently in cool water with pH-neutral soap or a tiny amount of gentle eco dishwashing liquid then dry it in the shade.

<u>NOTE:</u> Different trees give different dye colours. As long as you know it's not poisonous, experiment with leaves from local trees to see which give you colour. When the leaves of a tree stain the footpath, it's a good sign of a high tannin content and therefore a good dye plant. Silver eucalyptus leaves give good colour, as do oak leaves. Gather leaves respectfully and with permission from Traditional Owners.

You can also try:

*   onion skins (red or yellow)
*   turmeric
*   passionfruit skins
*   avocado pits or skins
*   pomegranate skins
*   tea leaves
*   rose leaves
*   hibiscus flowers

Not all natural dyes are long-lasting, but over-dyeing with a new colour once you get sick of the current one is easy to do and gives you endless options.

LET OUT A WAISTBAND

||||||||||||||||||||||||||||||||||||||||||||||||||||||||||||

I do this alteration to many of my own pairs of pants. It's nearly impossible to find clothes in standard sizes that fit our bodies perfectly. For instance, my hips and waist don't seem to go in or out at the right places to fit standard sizing. Here's how I take control of the fit and customise my clothes to make them just right.

Difficulty rating:
Medium

Time needed:
3 hours

What to upcycle: For the insert – old jeans, drill cotton pants or any fabric scrap of a similar weight to the item you're repairing

What you'll need

Tape measure

40 x 20 cm (16 x 8 inch) fabric scrap in a colour that works with your garment

Erasable fabric marker

Ruler

Quick unpick tool

Pins

Sewing machine

Threads

1. To figure out how much bigger your pants need to be, first measure your waist. Do this after lunch and be relaxed when you do it. This is so your alteration gives you enough room to breathe and stays comfortable.

Then measure the closed waistband of your garment from the inside from start to finish. The difference between these two measurements is how much bigger your pants need to be. We'll call this measurement A.

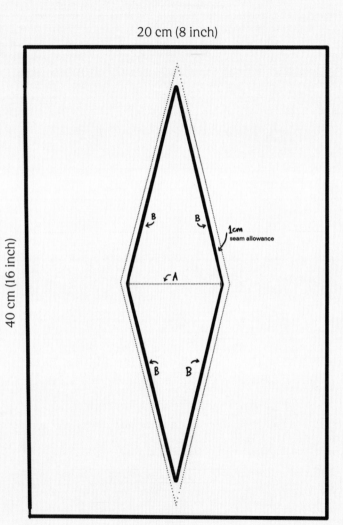

20 cm (8 inch)

40 cm (16 inch)

1cm
seam allowance

diagram not to scale

Mark these measurements on your piece of fabric:

A = how much bigger your pants need to be

B = measurement A x 3

For example, if your pants need to be 5 cm (2 inches) bigger, A = 5 cm (2 inches), B = 15 cm (6 inches).

After marking these measurements, add 1 cm (⅓ inch) all the way around for seam allowance. Once it's marked, cut out the diamond shape.

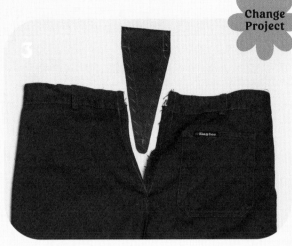

2. Unpick the centre back seam of your garment the same length as measurement B and cut through the centre back of the waistband. If there are belt loops, unpick these and set them aside for later. With your marker and ruler, mark 1 cm (⅓ inch) seam allowance down both sides of the split centre back.

3. Fold your piece of fabric in half along line A, with the right side of the fabric facing outwards. This triangle should fit neatly into the space you have opened in the centre back of the pants.

Stitch belt loop back on here

4. Pin your insert into the split, making sure the top edges of the pants line up with the top of your insert.

5. Stitch along the pinned edge. Iron so the seam allowances are extending into the garment, then stitch a line 5 mm (¼ inch) from the edge of the insert through all layers. Stitch your belt loop back onto the centre of the inserted panel.

The 'Change' pile   161

FRANKENSHIRT FROM OLD JEANS

This simple top is a great way to make use of your old jeans once you've patched them so many times that they're more patch than jean. Most jeans wear out in the same places; crotch, knees and bottom, leaving a lot of usable fabric in other areas, such as the backs of the legs and below the knees. Here is how to make use of that fabric.

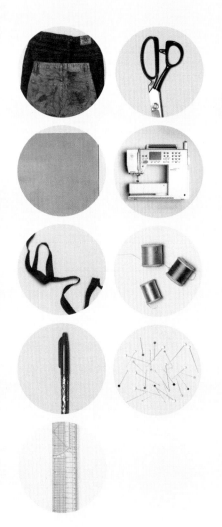

Difficulty rating:
Medium

Time needed:
3 hours

What to upcycle: Jeans, or light cotton or linen bedsheets for a summer-weight frankenshirt.

NOTE: The measurements listed here make a shirt that fits a chest measurement up to 116 cm (45½ inches). See page 166 for how to adjust sizing.

What you'll need

2 pairs of old jeans in different colours

60 x 60 cm (24 x 24 inch) paper to draw your pattern

2 pieces of cotton tape, each 2 m (6½ feet) long

Erasable fabric marker

Ruler

Scissors

Sewing machine

Thread

Pins

1. Draw two rectangles on your sheet of paper, 22 x 50 cm (9 x 20 inches) wide x long. On one rectangle, draw a line like the one marked in red on the diagram – it doesn't need to be exact.

Cut out the rectangles, then cut along the red line, discarding the piece shaded in grey.

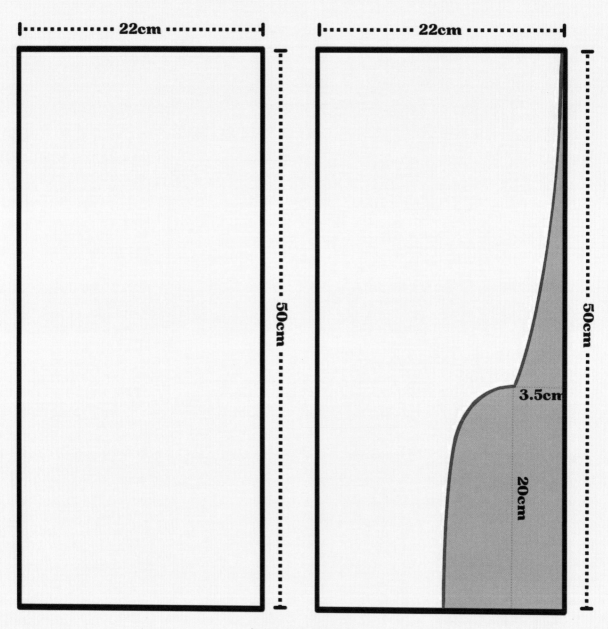

patterns not to scale

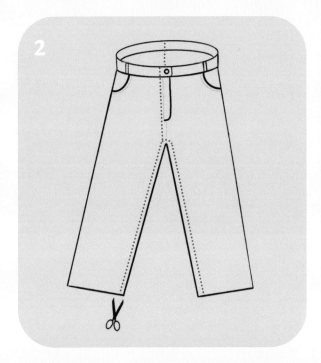

Change
Project

2. Lay the first pair of jeans flat. Cut up the inside seam of one leg and down the other side until it is completely separated. Cut through the centre front of the jeans, avoiding the zip and buttons. Cut through the centre back of the jeans.

3. Repeat the process on the second pair of jeans. Open these out and lay them flat. You now have four separate pieces of fabric.

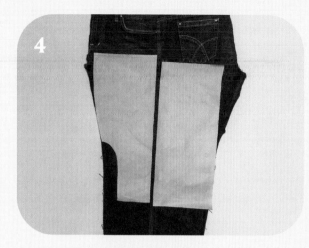

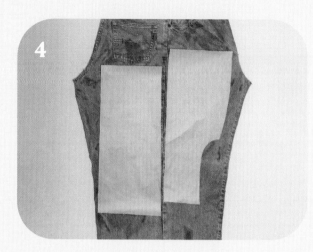

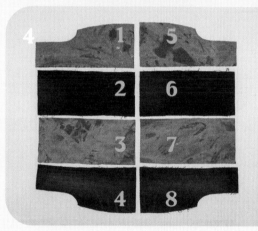

- To increase the size of the frankenshirt, add another panel of fabric to each side, front and back. To add to the length, make your panels longer than 50 cm (20 inches). The panel measurements listed in these instructions will fit chest measurements up to 116 cm (45½ inches).

4. Pin your pattern pieces onto the jeans and cut two of each pattern. Then flip the patterns over and cut two more of each. You'll end up with eight pieces in total. Lay out all your pieces as pictured above to make sure you've cut the right number of shapes.

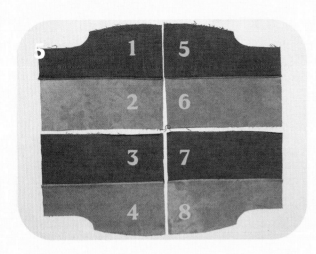

5. With the right sides of the fabric together, join panel 1 to 2, panel 3 to 4, panel 5 to 6 and panel 7 to 8.

6. Pin the centre seam together and sew.

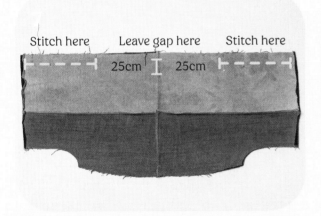

Stitch here   Leave gap here   Stitch here
25cm   25cm

7. Pin your new panels together (as pictured) with the right sides of the fabric facing inwards. Measure and mark 25 cm (10 inches) from the shoulder seam on each panel. Pin and sew a seam from this mark out to each edge.

8. Once stitched, the shape of the shirt should look like this.

The 'Change' pile   **167**

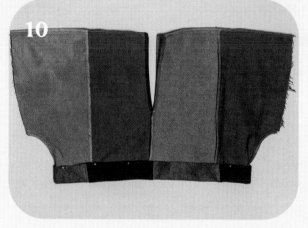

9. Fold your top in half along the shoulder seam, then pin and stitch the side seams. Roll the edges of the neckline over twice (1 cm/⅓ inch each roll), then pin and stitch for a finished edge.

10. Iron up the hem by 1 cm (⅓ inch) then another 5 cm (2 inches). Pin then stitch.

11. Once the hem is stitched, unpick a small 2 cm (1 inch) opening in each side seam.

With a safety pin in the end of your cotton tape, thread it through the channel created by the hem and out the other side seam.

12. Gather the cotton tape at each side seam and tie it
to your desired size.

- For fringing on the shoulders of the shirt and to save yourself some sewing, make your pattern panels 15 cm (6 inches) longer. Cut the extra 15 cm (6 inches) into strips and tie the strips together to create the shoulder seam, rather than sewing.

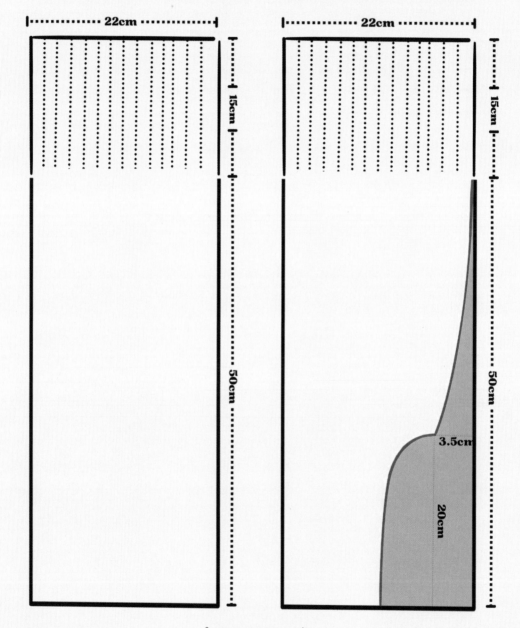

patterns not to scale

WORKWEAR APRON FROM OLD SHIRTS

IIIIIIIIIIIIIIIIIIIIIIIIIIIIIIIIIIIIIIIIIIIIIIIIIIIIIIIIIIIIIIIIIIIIIIIIIIIIIIIIIIIIIIIIIIIIIIIIIIIIIIIIIIIIIIIII

If your work is messy, this apron is a great coverall to keep you clean and looking snazzy, with all the pocket space you'll need to keep your tools close for easy access. Start with a shirt that is your size or larger.

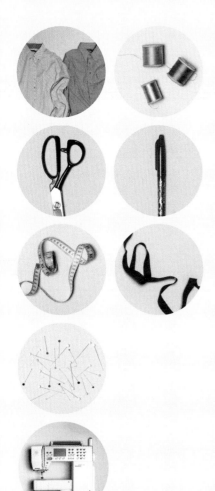

Difficulty rating:
Advanced

Time needed:
4 hours

What to upcycle: Worn-out collared shirts

What you'll need

2 old shirts

Scissors

Tape measure

Pins

Sewing machine

Thread

Erasable fabric marker

Cotton tape, 3 metres
(10 feet) long

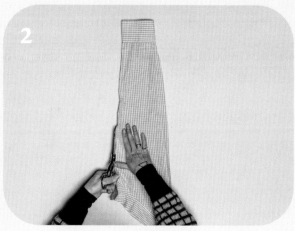

1. Lay your shirt flat and cut off each sleeve, making the sleeve openings large enough so you can wear layers under your apron. Cut off the collar around its base. Cut off the buttons and save them for another project.

2. Cut off the cuffs and along the bottom seam of each sleeve to open it out.

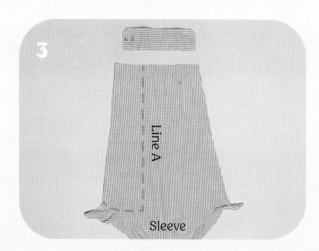

3. Place the opened sleeve underneath the centre front of the shirt at line A. Pin it in place, then stitch along line A using a straight machine stitch.

174 Keep

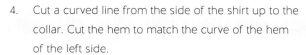

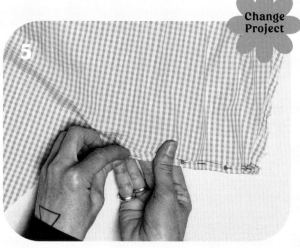

4. Cut a curved line from the side of the shirt up to the collar. Cut the hem to match the curve of the hem of the left side.

5. Double-roll all cut edges 1 cm (⅓ inch) and stitch them.

6. Pin then stitch cotton tape to the points of the shirt as pictured above to achieve a wrap-around effect.

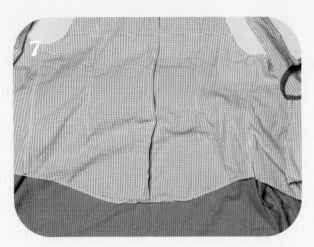

7. If you need to add extra length to your apron for more coverage, use another old shirt. Colour-blocking looks great for this. Pin the second shirt to the hem of your apron, stitch that line, then cut off the excess.

8. Cut pockets from your leftover sleeve fabric. A good size is 18 x 25 cm (7 x 10 inches), including seam allowance. Press 1 cm (⅓ inch) of each edge down, double-roll and stitch the top edge to hem it. Place the pocket anywhere on the apron that will be useful, stitching down both sides and the bottom edge.

SUN HAT FROM FABRIC SCRAPS

||||||||||||||||||||||||||||||||||||||||||||||||||||||||||||||||||||||||||||||||||

What better way to protect yourself from the sun than with this beautiful sun hat, made from your most colourful fabric scraps?

Difficulty rating:
Advanced

Time needed:
4 hours

What you'll need

Tape measure

String

Erasable fabric marker

70 x 70 cm (27½ x 27½ inch) paper

Thumbtack

Pencil

Paper scissors

Fabric scraps

Scissors

Pins

Sewing machine

<u>What to upcycle:</u> Small, colourful fabric scraps for the top layer, and colourful clothing or used denim for the heavier base layer

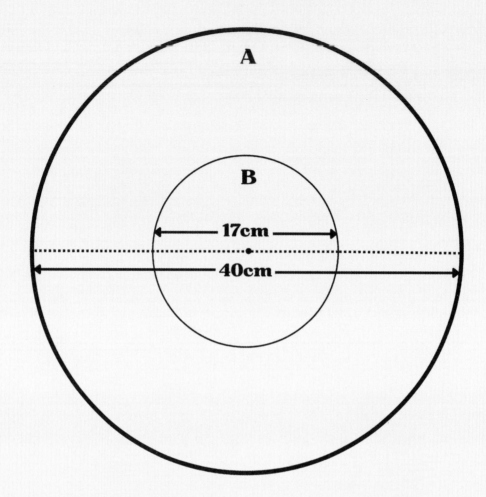

1. Draw a 17 cm (7 inch) diameter circle on your paper. Using the same centre point, draw a larger circle around it with a diameter of 40 cm (16 inches). Use your ruler to mark 1 cm (⅓ inch) on each side of the inner circle. These are the pattern pieces for the brim (piece A) and top (piece B) of your hat. Cut out the patterns for piece A and B.

2. Draw two curved parallel lines 10.5 cm (4 inches) apart. (To do this, tie a piece of string 70 cm/ 27½ inches around a pencil, and pin the other end of the string to a table with a thumbtack. Decrease the string length by 10.5 cm/4 inches to draw the other line.) Mark the centre of both curved lines then mark 24.5 cm (9½ inches) either side of the top centreline and 30 cm (11 ¾ inches) either side of the bottom centreline. Rule lines to join the top line to the bottom line. This is the pattern for your hat band (piece C), which includes 1 cm (⅓ inch) seam allowance on each edge. Cut out the pattern for piece C.

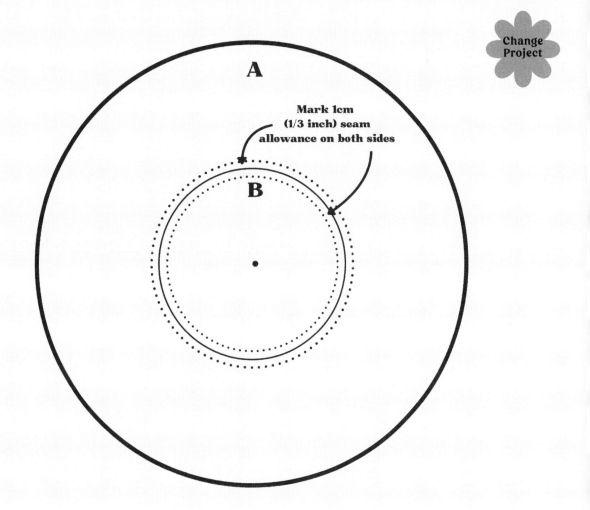

A

Mark 1cm (1/3 inch) seam allowance on both sides

B

*Pattern C includes all seam allowances

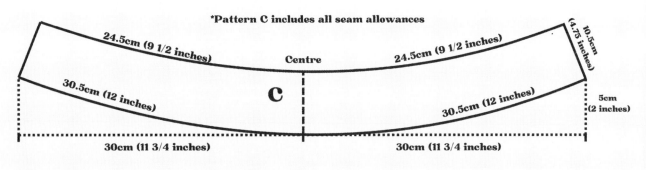

24.5cm (9 1/2 inches)

Centre

24.5cm (9 1/2 inches)

10.5cm (4.75 inches)

30.5cm (12 inches)

C

30.5cm (12 inches)

5cm (2 inches)

30cm (11 3/4 inches)

30cm (11 3/4 inches)

*patterns not to scale

NOTE: These measurements make a hat that fits a head circumference up to 60 cm (23½ inch).

3. Pin each pattern piece onto your base fabric and
    cut them out.

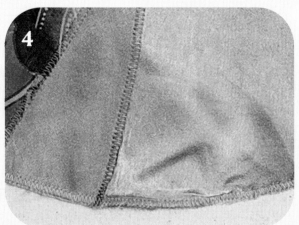

4. Pin your colourful fabric scraps onto the hat brim,
    then stitch them on using a zigzag stitch. Trim and
    zigzag stitch the inner and outer edges of this circle.

5. With right sides facing inwards, stitch the ends of the rectangular piece together using a straight stitch with 1 cm (⅓ inch) seam allowance then iron the seam allowance open.

6. Pin then stitch piece B onto piece C using a straight stitch.

7. Pin then stitch piece A onto piece C using a straight stitch.

- To make the hat reversible, cut an extra pair of pattern pieces A and B, and stitch them together following the directions in step 6. Turn back and iron 1 cm (⅓ inch) seam allowance around the base of piece C, then turn it inside out and stitch it inside the existing hat band.

- Experiment with borders on your brim, or for a more advanced project, bind the edges with bias tape.

FOOTREST OR DOGGY BED

||||||||||||||||||||||||||||||||||||||||||||||||||||||||||||||||||||||||||||||||

This project will make a footrest or a doggy bed that's 45 centimetres (17¾ inches) wide and 35 centimetres (13¾ inches) high, but you can alter these dimensions easily to make it the perfect size for your space or dog!

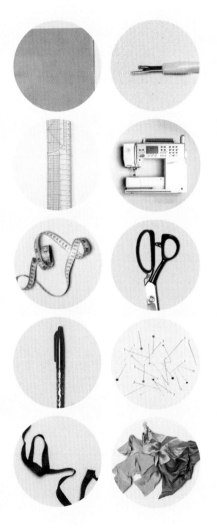

Difficulty rating:
Medium

Time needed:
3 hours

What to upcycle: Old curtains and upholstery fabric, heavy fabric scraps like canvas or denim, old wax cloth, or tent fabric. Stuff this project with clothes, sheets, pillows or doonas that are no longer usable.

What you'll need

Pattern paper 150 cm x 150 cm (59 x 59 inches)

Ruler

Tape measure

Erasable fabric marker

Cotton tape 150 cm (59 inches) long

3 fabric pieces – A: 50 cm x 50 cm (19¾ x 19¾ inches), B: 150 cm x 40 cm (59 x 15¾ inches), C: 150 cm x 30 cm (59 x 12 inches)

Quick unpick tool

Sewing machine

Scissors

Pins

Fabric scraps or old clothes, for stuffing

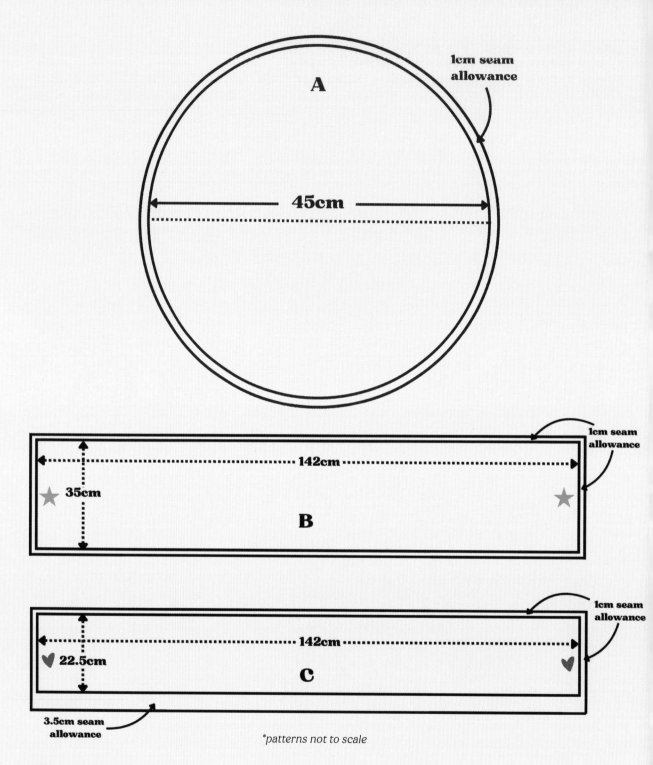

A

1cm seam
allowance

45cm

142cm

35cm

B

1cm seam
allowance

142cm

22.5cm

C

1cm seam
allowance

3.5cm seam
allowance

*patterns not to scale

1. Draw a circle with diameter 45 cm (17¾ inches) on your paper. Add 1 cm (⅓ inch) seam allowance around the whole circumference as pictured in the diagram. This is pattern piece A.

2. Draw a rectangle with measurements 142 cm x 35 cm (56 x 13¾ inches) on the paper. Add 1 cm (⅓ inch) seam allowance around the outside as pictured in the diagram. This is pattern piece B.

3. Draw a rectangle with measurements 142 cm x 22.5 cm (56 x 9 inches) on the paper. Add 1 cm (⅓ inch) seam allowance to both sides and the top edge. Add 3.5 cm (1⅓ inches) seam allowance to the bottom edge as pictured in the diagram. This is pattern piece C.

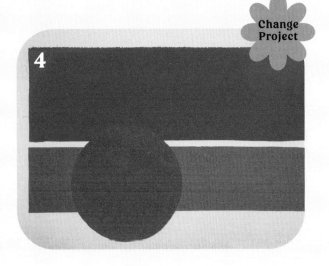

4. Cut out your patterns then pin them onto your fabric and cut them out. If your fabric pieces aren't big enough, this is the perfect opportunity to patch together heavier-weight scrap fabrics like old jeans or workwear clothing to create a tough, washable surface. (For more on how to join fabric pieces, see page 55.)

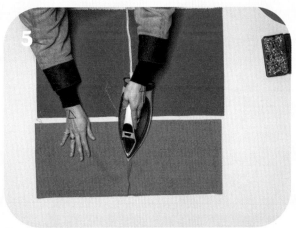

5. Fold each rectangle in half with right sides of the fabric together, matching the edges marked with stars for piece B and hearts for piece C. Pin and stitch these edges separately, with 1 cm (⅓ inch) seam allowance using a straight stitch. Iron seam allowances open.

The 'Change' pile 189

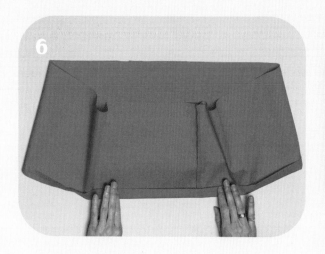

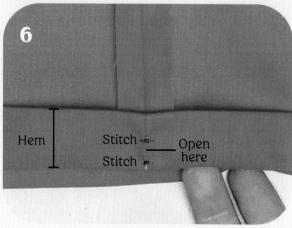

6. Turn back then iron 1 cm (⅓ inch) then 2.5 cm (1 inch) of the bottom edge of piece C. Pin this in place.

Within the 2.5 cm (1 inch) border, at the place where the fabric meets, make an opening of 1 cm (⅓ inch) with the quick unpick and secure each end of this opening with three small hand stitches.Stitch your pinned edge with a straight stitch all the way around, closing the channel.

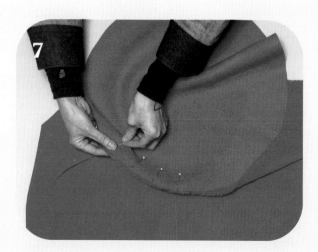

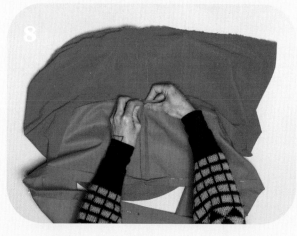

7. Pin piece A to the top of piece B, with right sides of the fabric facing inwards. Stitch these together with a straight stitch leaving 1 cm (⅓ inch) seam allowance.

8. Pin the bottom edge of piece B to the top edge of piece C, with right sides of the fabric facing each other. Stitch these together with a straight stitch, leaving 1 cm (⅓ inch).

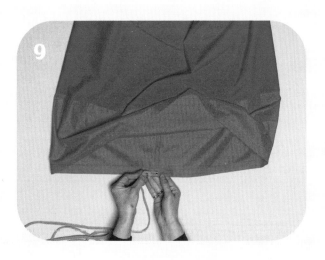

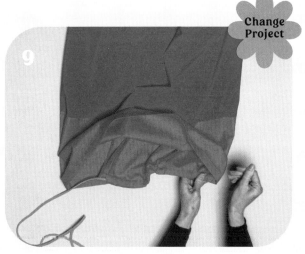

9. Using a safety pin, thread the cotton tape into the
    opening you've made in the channel. Pull it all the
    way through and out the other side, then tie both
    ends of the cotton tape together in a knot. Turn
    your footrest right side out.

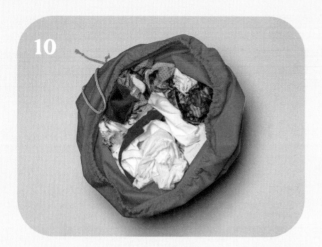

10. Now your footrest is ready to be stuffed full of clean fabric scraps and old clothes. Cut everything into smaller scraps for a smooth, not lumpy, filling.

NOTE: If you want a washable cover, make the same shape twice and put one cover inside the other. Then you can remove the outer layer when it's washing time.

POTATO PRINT VEGGIE BAGS

||||||||||||||||||||||||||||||||||||||||||||||||||||||||||||||||||||||||||||||||||||||||||||||||||||

You won't need plastic bags in the fruit and veg section of the supermarket once you've made these beauties. These bags are quick and easy to make, and if you print a design on the front of each one, they also serve as a great reminder for what to buy.

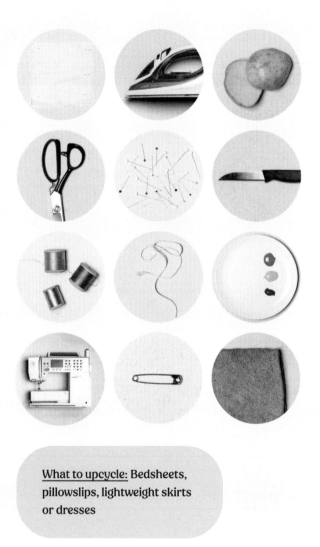

Difficulty rating:
Easy

Time needed:
1 hour

What you'll need

60 x 30 cm (24 x 12 inch) natural fibre fabric scrap (lightweight fabric is better so you aren't paying for it at the checkout)

Scissors

Thread

Sewing machine

Iron

Pins

60 cm (24 inch) piece of string

Safety pin

Large potato

Small, sharp knife

Fabric paint

Plate

Towel

What to upcycle: Bedsheets, pillowslips, lightweight skirts or dresses

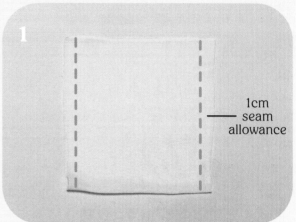

1cm
seam
allowance

1. Fold your fabric in half to make a 30 cm (12 inch)
   square. Stitch down each side with a straight stitch,
   leaving 1 cm (⅓ inch) seam allowance.

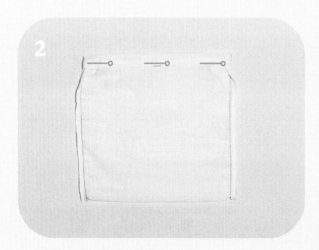

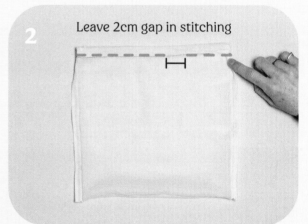

Leave 2cm gap in stitching

2. Fold 1 cm (⅓ inch) of the top edge down and iron it
   flat, then fold another 1.5 cm (½ inch) of the top edge
   down and iron it flat, forming a channel. Pin along
   the edge of this channel as pictured above, then
   stitch it all the way around, leaving a 2 cm (¾ inch)
   gap from where you started.

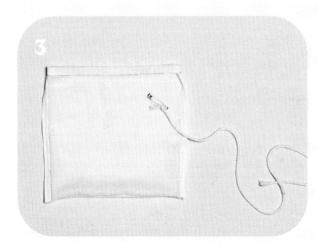

3. Tie your string or fabric strip onto the safety pin and thread it through the channel. Once it's out the other side, adjust so it's even on both sides then tie the two ends of string together in a knot.

4. Turn your bag right side out and iron it flat.

5. Cut the potato in half and use a paperclip to sketch out a type of fruit or vegetable that's usually on your shopping list. Using the knife, cut away the background of the design, leaving only the fruit or vegetable shape.

6. Pour a small amount of fabric paint onto a plate. Press your potato into the paint then stamp onto the produce bag. Make sure you test your print on a piece of scrap fabric before printing onto your finished bag. To get a clear print, it helps to have a flat towel or tea towel underneath the bag to make the printing surface a bit springy, and smooth the fabric nice and flat, without any wrinkles. Let your paint dry naturally then heat-set your fabric paint with an iron before washing.

7. Make a bag for each type of fruit or veg you usually buy at the market. What a beautiful shopping list!

CHAPTER 16: THE 'PASS IT ON' PILE

The 'Pass it on' pile is for items you've decided you definitely don't want to keep. They might be items you've grown out of, or things you haven't worn for more than a year and don't see yourself wearing again.

With clothing that's clean, in good condition and not in need of repair

- Sell it online to make some cash.

- Donate it to charity.

- Take it to a clothes swap.

- Donate it to a friend (making sure they actually want it first).

- Put it in the dress-up box at home or ask your local day-care or school if they have a dress-up box they're accepting donations for.

I want to emphasise the *good condition* part of this. If you're passing things on, they need to be in excellent condition. Charity shops spend far too much time and money disposing of donated items that aren't sale-worthy. The simple truth is that items you donate in poor condition will most likely end up in landfill. So don't make your rubbish someone else's responsibility. If you feel too guilty to throw it out, it probably wasn't the right thing to purchase in the first place. You'll need to hang on to it until you find a better option for recycling.

Unfortunately, there aren't a lot of options for poor-quality synthetic items. Think about this before buying them, because they might end up being a responsibility you're not willing to take on.

With clothing that's too far gone to wear, repair or donate

Textile recycling

A growing list of companies now accept textiles for recycling, even damaged and worn-out items. These items need to be *clean* and you need to check each company's list of what they will and won't accept. Textile recyclers vary in terms of how and what they recycle, but often items in good and wearable condition will be redistributed to charities. Unwearable items may be turned into new textiles – the technology for this is constantly improving.

Down-filled items can be tricky to recycle, as are clothing items containing wire, but if you do some digging, some programs can accept these items. You can also separate things like underwire out of bras yourself. Just cut through the end of the channel containing the wire and push it out. Bras without underwire are accepted by many textile recyclers. If your down-filled item can no longer function as clothing, think about using it as pet bedding or floor cushions. Use it to stuff the footrest project (see pages 187–192). At the very end of its life, you can compost 100% down filling at home; just make sure there's no polyfill mixed in and remove any synthetic fabric and trims. Once the down is emptied, you could send what's left to textile recycling as long as it's completely cleaned out.

Try to support those companies that are turning textiles into high-quality new fabrics that are themselves recyclable, rather than downcycling fabrics into industrial rags or similar. Downcycling means the product created has lower quality and functionality than the original product. Industrial rags, for example, end up in landfill after one use, so we want to avoid this and instead turn our textile waste into products that can be reused, remanufactured and kept out of landfill forever.

If there's a cost for a textile recycling service, it's a small price to pay for someone else to take responsibility for your textile waste and commit to keeping it out of landfill. That deserves millions! A service you pay for is more likely to have the funds to recycle your textiles into quality new fabrics.

The process of textile recycling requires energy, transport, chemicals and water, so despite these companies doing fantastic work, it's not an entirely guilt-free option. We need to make sure we require the services of textile recyclers as little as possible.

Compost

In theory, natural fibres can be composted, but you need to remove tags, buttons, zips and interfacing first. The threads that stitch our clothes together usually contain polyester, so remove them if you're not certain they're made from natural fibres. Natural-fibre clothes are sometimes dyed with synthetic chemicals or contain mixed fibres. So before you compost, check that you're throwing in a piece of natural fibre, not a mixture of plastics. Keep clothing compost away from food crops if you're unsure about the content.

Add to your bag of fabric scraps

Items beyond repair can be kept as handy fabric scraps for mending jobs. Most projects listed in this book require fabric scraps, so keep a bag of scraps with lots of different types of fabric for different types of repairs. You never know when you'll need them!

You can also use fabric scraps for cleaning cloths around the house, as ties for the plants in your veggie garden, or as string and ribbons for your craft projects. Stuff them into your bean bag or cushions when they need a boost.

What can go in the bin?

While I want to tell you that nothing should go into the bin, there are issues associated with old clothing carrying possible hygiene risks (e.g. used underwear and cloth nappies), which means these items can't be donated or recycled. These items can still be used as fabric scraps for cleaning up spills at home, once you've given them a good wash and left them in the sun, but don't donate or recycle them unless the companies specifically state they can accept them. These items are perfect to use in the footrest project (see pages 187–192).

For all other textile items, you'll find there is usually a way to keep most things out of landfill. Keep checking in with your local textile recyclers to find out what they accept. Because technology is constantly improving, the list of what can be recycled is constantly being added to.

Think before you buy

Before you buy an item, think about what will happen when it reaches the end of its useful life in its current form. If you don't know what you'll be able to do with it, do your research before you buy it, and have a plan for when you get there. If it can't be recycled, remade or composted, it needs to be redesigned. Don't buy it.

ORGANISE A CLOTHING SWAP

||||||||||||||||||||||||||||||||||||||||||||||||||||||||||||||||||||||||||||||||||

Organising a clothing swap lets you score clothes guilt-free, minus the price tag. A good clothing swap can redistribute your loved pieces of clothing, saving them from landfill and filling gaps in your wardrobe, all without costing a cent. They are a wonderful way of bringing people together for a communal game of dress-ups.

Difficulty rating:
Easy

Time needed:
1 week

What you'll need

Venue

Event promotion materials

Coat hangers

Steamer (optional)

Tokens (optional)

Clothing racks

Tables

Chairs

Room dividers or change-room facilities

Full-length mirror

Music

Oil burner and essential oils

Refreshments (optional)

Nametags (optional)

Place/charity to donate leftover clothing items

Venue

First, you'll need to decide on a venue for your clothes swap. How big do you want it to be? Do you want it to be you and your group of friends, or extend it wider? A bigger pool of people means a wider range of clothes to swap. You could host a small group of friends at home, but bigger groups need more space. When considering options, think about the weather and the comfort of people trying on clothes. Outdoors might seem like a good idea but you'll need a backup plan. Local councils usually have halls for hire at reasonable rates. Your local scout hall or school hall could be good options.

Promotion

Whether your swap is big or small, you'll need to spend some time promoting it and reminding people to attend. You'll need an initial social media post or poster/flyers, as well as multiple reminders leading up to the date. Ask people to RSVP so you can collect a list of email addresses for reminders.

What to accept

Set the parameters for swapping early and communicate them clearly. Some swaps limit the amount of clothing to 10 pieces per person to make assessing the pieces easy when people arrive. Always ask people to bring clean items in a condition they'd be happy giving to their best friend as a gift. Steaming or ironing clothes beforehand and bringing them on hangers also helps to speed things up and will make the swap look amazing.

Trading system

Decide on a system for trading – you can use tokens or an honesty system. If you have enough time and/or people to help you, have someone assess pieces as they're brought in, then give out a token for each item of clothing contributed. This token can be 'spent' on an equivalent item of clothing. A pure wool winter coat might be worth three tokens whereas a singlet top is worth one.

Presentation

The way clothes look at a swap is important. Their presentation affects the value participants place on clothes, even when they're free! Clutter is instantly overwhelming, so make the swap look open, tidy and accessible. For this reason, provide clothing racks, hangers, tables and chairs. All these can be loaned and returned, so there's no need to buy anything new. Ask on your local community's Facebook page.

Avoid piles of wrinkled clothes on the ground. Hang clothes on racks or fold them on tables. Having a clothes steamer for participants to give things a quick steam before they go on display will make a big difference to how the garments are perceived.

Think about the stores you like shopping in and how they display clothes. You want enough light to see clothes clearly; also play some music and burn essential oils so everything smells good. If you can borrow a couple of shop mannequins for the event, dress them up. Make the atmosphere friendly and inviting.

Creating a visual flow with colour, and arranging clothes by type, like merchandising in a store, can help people move through the space. Ensure there's enough space on racks to see items clearly. Set up a change room with room dividers or provide a dry, comfortable and private place for people to try things on in front of a full-length mirror.

Extras

You could consider providing food and drinks, or get people to contribute refreshments. Some swaps encourage participants to wear nametags and do icebreakers to get everyone involved and meeting people.

What to do with what's left

Decide early on what you'll do with leftover items from the swap. You can use this as part of your promotion. A good cause at the end of the swap will encourage attendees to bring good-quality gear and be willing to leave it with you to donate afterwards.

CHAPTER 17: KEEP YOUR WARDROBE FRESH

Congratulations! You have officially loved your wardrobe back to life! You should be excited about every single item in your wardrobe and feeling satisfied that you've taken care of your clothing needs for a long time to come.

It's important to keep your clothes in circulation so you always know what you have, can make use of it, and stay on top of maintenance and repair. Doing this means you won't waste what you have and, most importantly, it will help you avoid the temptation to buy more. If you ever feel things are getting out of hand, revisit the clothing calculator and wardrobe stocktake projects (see pages 18–23) to get your head around what you need and have, and repeat the wardrobe revolution project (see page 107) to breathe new life into what you already own.

One way to keep what you own fresh in your mind is by downloading an outfit-planning app. This lets you photograph your clothes and curate them into outfits digitally. It helps you keep track of how often you wear each item and will let you know if you're neglecting something. Neglected items might need to be transformed or passed on.

Project: Keep it in circulation

Invite a friend over to help with this project. It's similar to the style play project (see pages 28–33), but you can do this one at home with your own clothes.

Select your favourite item of clothing and curate five different outfits combining that piece with items you wear less often. Take photos of each look, even ones you wouldn't usually try. This will help you break out of your comfort zone.

Keep doing this with different key pieces until you've got about 21 good outfit ideas – that's three weeks of outfits you don't have to think about. Collaborate with your friend on this. Chances are they'll put things together in ways you'd never considered.

Print out the photos of your favourite outfits and stick them on the wall close to your wardrobe. This is the best way to remember what you own. It also stops you reaching for the same three items, day after day. You'll have outfit inspiration on tap when you're in a rush getting dressed in the morning.

LIST OF PROJECTS

RESOURCES /FURTHER READING

Books on natural dyeing

Jenny Dean, *Wild Colour*, Mitchell Beazley, 1999.

India Flint, *Eco Colour*, Allen and Unwin, 2008.

Books on mending and repair

Flora Collingwood-Norris, *Visible Creative Mending for Knitwear*, Collingwood-Norris, 2021.

Jessica Marquez, *Make and Mend*, Octopus, 2019.

Molly Martin, *The Art of Repair*, Octopus, 2021.

Celia Pym, *On Mending*, Quickthorn Books, 2022.

Katrina Rodabaugh, *Mending Matters*, Abrams Inc., 2018.

Books on sewing

Winifred Aldrich, *Metric Pattern Cutting for Men's Wear* (5th edition), Wiley, 2011.

Winifred Aldrich, *Metric Pattern Cutting for Women's Wear* (6th edition), Wiley, 2015.

Assembil Books, *How Patterns Work*, Assembil Books, 2024.

Assembil Books, *How to Start Sewing*, Assembil Books, 2016.

Books on sustainable fashion and design

Jonathan Chapman, *Emotionally Durable Design* (2nd edition), Routledge, 2005.

Orsola de Castro, *Loved Clothes Last*, Penguin Books, 2021.

Kate Fletcher, *Sustainable Fashion and Textiles*, Earthscan, 2008.

Alison Gwilt, *A Practical Guide to Sustainable Fashion* (2nd Edition), Bloomsbury Publishing, 2020.

Alison Gwilt, Alice Payne and Evelise Anicet Ruthschilling (eds.), *Global Perspectives on Sustainable Fashion*, Bloomsbury Publishing, 2019.

Clare Press, *The Wardrobe Crisis*, Black Inc., 2016.

Clare Press, *Wear Next*, Thames and Hudson Australia, 2023.

Sofi Thanhauser, *Worn*, Penguin Books, 2022.

Lucianne Tonti, *Sundressed*, Black Inc., 2022.

Apps

Stylebook

Good On You

Web resources

Australian Fashion Council
ausfashioncouncil.com

Centre for Sustainable Fashion
sustainable-fashion.com

Clean Clothes Campaign
cleanclothes.org

Collective Fashion Justice
collectivefashionjustice.org

Ethical Clothing Australia
ethicalclothingaustralia.org.au

Ellen Macarthur Foundation
ellenmacarthurfoundation.org

Fashion Revolution
fashionrevolution.org

Fibershed
fibershed.org

Good On You
goodonyou.eco

Kate Fletcher
katefletcher.com

The Environmental Justice Foundation
ejfoundation.org

Remake Our World
remake.world

ABOUT THE AUTHOR

Leah Giblin is a textile and clothing designer, educator, and sustainable fashion advocate.

Her clothing label, Day Keeper, is designed and made in Sydney, Australia. Leah's educational focus on mending, natural dyeing and upcycling has seen her deliver workshops through museums, schools, councils and festivals. Leah currently teaches fashion and textiles at the University of New South Wales, Sydney.

With a focus on sustainability and the elimination of textile waste, Leah champions care and repair, with the goal of helping people navigate clothing ownership. She advocates for meaningful and long-lasting relationships with our clothes and for fashion that makes us feel good about ourselves, and is kind to the planet, to animals and to the people who make it.

ACKNOWLEDGEMENTS

Thank you to my beauties, Ailish and Tomas. To Killian for friendship always and shelter while I wrote this book. To Suze and Mike for supporting me in every creative endeavour and teaching me that making and mending is the way. To the very best sister, Erinna Annie, for reading, listening and giving me constant encouragement. To Alexandra for the same and for telling me the truth about writing books. To Agatha for your genius insights and always having my back. To Marianne for reading, and your exquisite sewing, patterns and support. To Verity, Shauna, Juliet and Lizzie for your love and care. To Morgan, Bec and Rochelle, thank you for the early conversations and ideas. To my brothers for letting me dress you up, and your wonderful families, thanks for cheering me on from afar.

Thank you to the incredible Mark Campbell, Rachel Dennis, Jess Cox and the HarperCollins team, for your gentle guidance, brilliant editing and encouragement. To the talented Bee Elton and Mietta Yans for magnificent images and design. To the shoot dream team, Marianne, Willow and Jai, we couldn't have done it without you, as well as Delia and Rose for those connections. Thank you to the talented Amber Moxey for your makeup and hair artistry.

To everyone we photographed, Agatha Gothe-Snape and Rolland Gothe-Snape-Cairns, Willow Kable, Jai Strachan, Morgan and Bec Marlow, Curly Fernandez, Megan Hanson, Darren Holt, Maya Abraham and Nicola Nelson, thank you.

Thank you Talia, Billie-Rose and Casablanca Marrickville, for letting us take photos in your beautiful shop. To Aggie and Mitch, Morgan and Bec for the same at your places, thank you. To Gail Rice for your valuable advice. To my beloved UNSW, SBS and Aisle 10 crews. To Marg, Hannah, Sophia and Brent for your help at the very start, I'm so grateful.

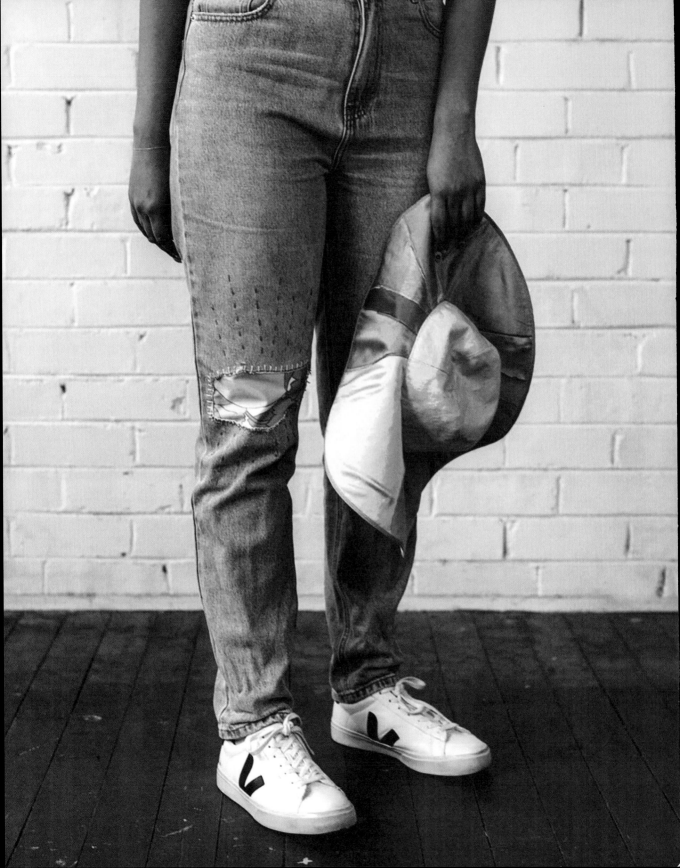

NOTES

1   Morgan McFall-Johnsen, 'These facts show how unsustainable the fashion industry is', World Economic Forum, 31 January 2020, https://www weforum.org/agenda/2020/01/fashion-industry-carbon-unsustainable-environment-pollution/

2   United Nations Economic Commission forEurope (UNECE), 'UN Alliance aims to put fashion on path to sustainability', UNECE Sustainable Development Goals, 2018, https://unece.org forestry/press/un-alliance-aims-put-fashion-path sustainability; United Nations Framework Convention on Climate Change (UNCCC), 'UN helps fashion industry shift to low carbon', UN Climate Change, 2018, https://unfccc.int/news/ un-helps-fashionindustry-shift-to-low-carbon

3   Elyse R. Stanes & Christopher R. Gibson, 'Materials that linger: An embodied geography of polyester clothes', 2017, https://ro.uow.edu.au/

4   Orsola de Castro, 'Continuing my update on a previous quote', *Instagram* post 23 May 2024, https://www.instagram.com/orsoladecastro/reel C7TbFw8IWBL/

5   Changing Markets Foundation, *Licence to greenwash: How certification schemes and voluntary initiatives are fuelling fossil fashion*, 2022, https://changingmarkets.org/report/licence-to-greenwash-how-certification-schemes-and-voluntary-initiatives-are-fuelling-fossil-fashion/

6   'How consumers can reduce returns', *Penn Today*, 6 January 2022, https://penntoday.upenn. edu/news/how-consumers-and-retailers-can-reduce-returns

7   Elle Penner, 'The ultimate guide: How to build your first capsule wardrobe', Modern Minimalism, https://modernminimalism.com/how-to-build-a-capsule-wardrobe/

8   Dimitri Weideli, *Environmental analysis of US online shopping*, thesis, Ecole Polytechnique Fédérale de Lausanne, 2013.

9   Kate Fletcher, 'Slow fashion: An invitation for systems change', *Fashion Practice*, vol.2, no.2, pp.259–265.

10   'Greenwashing', *Merriam-Webster dictionary*, https://www.merriam-webster.com/dictionary/ greenwashing

11   Changing Markets Foundation, Greenwash, 2022, https://greenwash.com/

12   Changing Markets Foundation, Greenwash, 2022, https://greenwash.com/

13   Changing Markets Foundation, Greenwash, 2022, https://greenwash.com/

14   Changing Markets Foundation, *Licence to greenwash: How certification schemes and voluntary initiatives are fuelling fossil fashion*, 2022, https://changingmarkets.org/report/licence-to-greenwash-how-certification-schemes-and-voluntary-initiatives-are-fuelling-fossil-fashion/

15   Changing Markets Foundation, *Licence to Greenwash: How certification schemes and voluntary initiatives are fuelling fossil fashion*, 2022, https://changingmarkets.org/report/licence-to-greenwash-how-certification-schemes-and-voluntary-initiatives-are-fuelling-fossil-fashion/

16   'More sustainable clothing brands: The 50 top-rated brands on Good on You', Good on You, 10 June 2024, https://goodonyou.eco/

17   Global Organic Textile Standards, https:// global-standard.org/

18   Social Accountability International, https://sa-intl.org/programs/sa8000/

19 PETA, 'All about PETA', https://www.peta.org/about-peta/learn-about-peta/

20 'About our standards', B Lab Global, https://www.bcorporation.net/en-us/standards/

21 'OEKO-TEX® standards enable everyone to make responsible decisions and protect natural resources', Global Organic Textile Standards, https://www.oeko-tex.com/en/our-standards

22 ThredUp, Fashion footprint calculator, 2024, https://www.thredup.com/fashionfootprint/

23 Hannah Marriott, 'The truth about fast fashion: Can you tell how ethical your clothing is by its price?', *The Guardian*, 29 July 2021, https://www.theguardian.com/fashion/2021/jul/29/the-truth-about-fast-fashion-can-you-tell-how-ethical-your-clothing-is-by-its-price

24 Walk Free, 'Stitched with slavery in the seams', Global Slavery Index, https://www.walkfree.org/global-slavery-index/findings/spotlights/stitched-with-slavery-in-the-seams/

25 Fashion Revolution, https://www.fashionrevolution.org/

26 Walk Free, 'Understanding the scale of modern slavery', Global Slavery Index, https://www.walkfree.org/global-slavery-index/

27 Matter of Trust, https://matteroftrust.org/

28 Jane Kwan, *Textilepedia: The complete fabric guide*, Fashionary International Ltd., 2023.

29 Jane Kwan, *Textilepedia: The complete fabric guide*, Fashionary International Ltd., 2023.

30 Ashlee Uren, 'Material guide: What is polyester and can it ever be sustainable?', Good on You, 18 March 2024, https://goodonyou.eco/how-sustainable-is-polyester/

31 Changing Markets Foundation, *Licence to Greenwash: How certification schemes and voluntary initiatives are fuelling fossil fashion*, 2022, https://changingmarkets.org/report/licence-to-greenwash-how-certification-schemes-and-voluntary-initiatives-are-fuelling-fossil-fashion/

32 Kirsten Brodde, 'What are microfibers and why are our clothes polluting the oceans?, Greenpeace, 2 March 2017, https://www.greenpeace.org/international/story/6956/what-are-microfibers-and-why-are-our-clothes-polluting-the-oceans/

33 Si Liu, JinHui Huang, Wei Zhang, LiXiu Shi, KaiXin Yi, HanBo Yu, ChenYu Zhang, SuZhou Li, JiaoNi Li, 'Microplastics as a vehicle of heavy metals in aquatic environments: A review of adsorption factors, mechanisms, and biological effects', *Journal of Environmental Management*, 2022, vol. 302, Part A, https://doi.org/10.1016/j.jenvman.2021.113995.

34 Julien Boucher & Damien Friot, *Primary microplastics in the oceans: A global evaluation of sources*, IUCN, 2017, https://portals.iucn.org/library/node/46622

35 Mary Catherine O'Connor, 'Inside the lonely fight against the biggest environmental problem you've never heard of', *The Guardian*, 28 October 2014, https://www.theguardian.com/sustainable-business/2014/oct/27/toxic-plastic-synthetic-microscopic-oceans-microbeads-microfibers-food-chain

36 Ashlee Uren, 'Material guide: What is polyester and can it ever be sustainable?', Good on You, 18 March 2024, https://goodonyou.eco/how-sustainable-is-polyester/

37 Elyse Stanes and Chris Gibson, 'Materials that linger: An embodied geography of polyester clothes', *Geoforum*, 2017, vol.85, pp.27–36, https://doi.org/10.1016/j.geoforum.2017.07.006

38 Adrienne Matei, 'Thread carefully: Your gym clothes could be leaching toxic chemicals', *The Guardian*, 2 November 2023, https://www.theguardian.com/wellness/2023/nov/02/workout-clothes-sweat-chemicals-cancer; Oddný Ragnarsdottir, Mohamed Abou-Elwafa Abdallah, & Stuart Harrad, 'Dermal bioavailability of perfluoroalkyl substances using *in vitro* 3D human skin equivalent models', *Environment International*, vol.188, art.108772, https://www.sciencedirect.com/science/article/pii/S0160412024003581

39 Wendy Graham, 'Are clothes made from recycled plastic actually eco-friendly?' Moral Fibres, 2 March 2024, https://moralfibres.co.uk/are-clothes-made-from-recycled-plastic-eco-friendly/

40 'Made-by environmental benchmark for fibres', Common Objective, 6 March 2018, https://www.commonobjective.co/article/made-by-environmental-benchmark-for-fibres

41 Jane Kwan, *Textilepedia: The complete fabric guide*, Fashionary International Ltd, 2023.

42 Federal Trade Commission (FTC) Bureau of Consumer Protection, 'How to avoid bamboozling your customers', FTC business alert, https://www.ftc.gov/system/files/documents/plain-language/alt172-how-avoid-bamboozling-your-customers.pdf

43 Lucianne Tonti, 'Rayon unravelled: Fashion's most confusing fibre has a dark past but hopeful future', *The Guardian*, 20 August 2022, https://www.theguardian.com/fashion/2022/aug/20/rayon-unravelled-fashions-most-confusing-fibre-has-a-dark-past-but-hopeful-future

44 Ellen Macarthur Foundation, *A new textiles economy; Redesigning fashion's future*, 2017, https://archive.ellenmacarthurfoundation.org/assets/downloads/A-New-Textiles-Economy.pdf

45 Don-Alvin Adegeest, 'Not sustainable: Over 300 million trees a year are logged to produce viscose', Fashion United, 5 July 2024, https://fashionunited.uk/news/fashion/not-sustainable-over-300-million-trees-a-year-are-logged-to-produce-viscose/2024070576492

46 Jennifer Okafor, 'Ramie fabric – what is ramie? Sustainability, pros, and cons', Trvst, 23 October 2023, https://www.trvst.world/sustainable-living/fashion/ramie-fabric-sustainability/; 'Made-by environmental benchmark for fibres', Common Objective, 6 March 2018, https://www.commonobjective.co/article/made-by-environmental-benchmark-for-fibres

47 'Made-by environmental benchmark for fibres', Common Objective, 6 March 2018, https://www.commonobjective.co/article/made-by-environmental-benchmark-for-fibres

48 Walk Free, 'Stitched with slavery in the seams', Global Slavery Index, https://www.walkfree.org/global-slavery-index/findings/spotlights/stitched-with-slavery-in-the-seams/

49 Woolmark, 'Wool as a sustainable fibre for textiles', https://www.woolmark.com/industry/sustainability/wool-is-a-sustainable-fibre/

50 RSPCA Australia, 'Mulesing: The welfare issue we need to be talking about', 21 April 2023, https://www.rspca.org.au/latest-news/blog/mulesing-welfare-issue-we-need-be-talking-about/

51 Helen X. Trejo and Tasha L. Lewis, 'Slow fashion and fiber farming: Nexus for community engagement', *Fashion Practice*, 2017, vol.9, no.1, pp.120–142, https://doiorg/10.1080/17569370.2016.1220544

52 Fibershed, https://fibershed.org/

53 'Silk', Encylopaedia Britannica, https://kids.britannica.com/students/article/silk/277065

54 Ellen MacArthur Foundation, *A new textiles economy: Redesigning fashion's future*, 2017, https://archive.ellenmacarthurfoundation.org/assets/downloads/A-New-Textiles-Economy.pdf

55 Council of Fashion Designers of America, 'Silk', https://cfda.com/resources/materials/detail/silk

56 Council of Fashion Designers of America, 'Silk', https://cfda.com/resources/materials/detail/silk

57 Emily Chan, 'How often should we wash our clothes, exactly?', *Vogue World*, 25 June 2023, https://www.vogue.com/article/how-often-should-we-wash-our-clothes

58 Choice Australia, 'Clothes washing symbols explained', 8 December 2021, https://www.choice.com.au/home-and-living/laundry-and-cleaning/washing-machines/articles/clothes-washing-symbols-explained

59 ecostore, 'Ingredient index', https://ecostore.com/au/ingredients/nasty

60 Andrew Krosofsky, 'How does laundry detergent affect the environment?', Green Matters, 2 November 2020, https://www.greenmatters.com/p/detergent-environmental-effects; Suaibu O. Badmus, Hussein K. Amusa, Tajudeen A. Oyehan and Tawfik A. Saleh, 'Environmental risks and toxicity of surfactants: Overview of analysis, assessment, and remediation techniques', *Environmental Science and Pollution Research International*, vol.28, no.44, pp.62058–62104, https://www.ncbi.nlm.nih.gov/pmc/articles/PMC8480275/

61 United States Department of Health and Human Services, National Toxicology Program, *Report on carcinogens, 13th edition*, 2014, https://downloads.regulations.gov/EPA-HQ-TRI-2015-0011-0004/content.pdf

62 Mark Hay, 'How dangerous are dry cleaning chemicals?', *Vice*, 6 June 2019, https://www.vice.com/en/article/kzmp7x/how-dangerous-are-dry-cleaning-chemicals

63 US Environmental Protection Agency, 'Reducing air pollution from: Dry cleaning operations', *Healthy air: A community and business guide*, 2005, https://www.epa.gov/sites/default/files/2017-06/documents/drycleaners_oo_sheet.pdf; Lucianne Tonti, 'Clean and green: How to pick a dry-cleaner that's good for the environment – and you', *The Guardian*, 12 July 2022, https://www.theguardian.com/lifeandstyle/2022/jul/12/clean-and-green-how-to-pick-a-dry-cleaner-thats-good-for-the-environment-and-you; NSW Environment Protection Authority, 'Dry cleaning chemicals', 14 July 2021, https://www.epa.nsw.gov.au/your-environment/chemicals/dry-cleaning-chemicals

64 Melanie Hearse, 'Do you really need a clothes dryer?', Choice Australia, 19 June 2019, https://www.choice.com.au/home-and-living/laundry-and-cleaning/dryers/articles/do-you-need-a-dryer

65 Judith Weis, 'Laundry is a top source of microplastic pollution – but you can clean your clothes more sustainably', ABC News, 15 January 2024, https://www.abc.net.au/news/2024-01-15/laundry-is-a-top-source-of-microplastic-pollution/103321100?utm_source=abc_news_app&utm_medium=content_shared&utm_campaign=abc_news_app&utm_content=air-drop

66 Lucianne Tonti, 'Jean therapy: Putting them in the freezer doesn't work – so how do you make jeans last?', *The Guardian*, 19 October 2021, https://www.theguardian.com/lifeandstyle/2021/oct/19/jean-therapy-putting-them-in-the-freezer-doesnt-work-so-how-do-you-make-jeans-last

First published in 2025 by Harper by Design
This edition published in 2025 by Smith Street Books
Naarm (Melbourne) | Australia
smithstreetbooks.com

ISBN: 978-1-9230-4994-9

Smith Street Books respectfully acknowledges the Wurundjeri People of the Kulin Nation,
who are the Traditional Owners of the land on which we work, and we pay our respects
to their Elders past and present.

Publisher: Mark Campbell
Senior editor: Rachel Dennis
Cover and internal design and layout: Mietta Yans
Photographer: Bee Elton

Printed & bound in China by 1010 Printing

Book 377
10 9 8 7 6 5 4 3 2 1